# Targeting Mental Maths

AUSTRALIAN CURRICULUM EDITION

Judy Tertini

PASCAL
PRESS

Targeting Mental Maths Year 2
Written by Judy Tertini

Reprinted 2010, 2011, 2012
**Updated in 2013 for the Australian Curriculum**
Reprinted 2014, 2015, 2016, 2017, 2018, 2019, 2021
**Updated in 2022 for the Australian Curriculum**
Reprinted 2023, 2024

ISBN 978 1 92288 724 5

Published by Pascal Press
PO Box 250
Glebe NSW 2037
(02) 9198 1748
www.pascalpress.com.au

Publisher: Katy Pike
Series Editor: Garda Turner
Editor: Amanda Santamaria
Designed and typeset by The Modern Art Production Group

Printed by Wai Man Book Binding (China) Ltd.

# Contents

# Introduction

## The importance of mental mathematics

The development of a variety of mental strategies helps to make children confident mathematicians.

Students who can perform mathematical computations swiftly and accurately in their heads are seen as being 'good at maths'. In general, poorer performing students use less efficient strategies and the development of mental computation through a strategy approach can help them move forwards. Research has shown that 'after instruction students seem more likely to use strategies that reflected number sense and that this was a long-term change.' (Markovits and Sowder, 1994)

The Year 2 Targeting Mental Maths book has been written to complement the Targeting Maths Australian Curriculum Year 2 Student Book. The two-page weekly units run parallel to the contents in the student book. Units are divided into four terms of work and each term ends with a Revision Unit. There are 32 units in total.

A unit consists of two facing pages. The left-hand page has three groups of quick mental exercises that constantly practise the necessary maths facts. The right-hand page always starts with an explanation and practice of a mental strategy. This is followed by exercises that include work on space, measurement, position, number, data, chance etc. The page concludes with a Problem of the week.

# Introduction

Students with number sense know the relative size of numbers and use a variety of computation strategies to solve a problem. This enables them to approach maths with a real sense of what they are being asked to do, making them more confident, with a greater ability to work mathematically.

Targeting Mental Maths fulfils the need for easily accessible mental warm-ups, constant practice of maths facts, a useful homework book and further revision of a concept being taught.

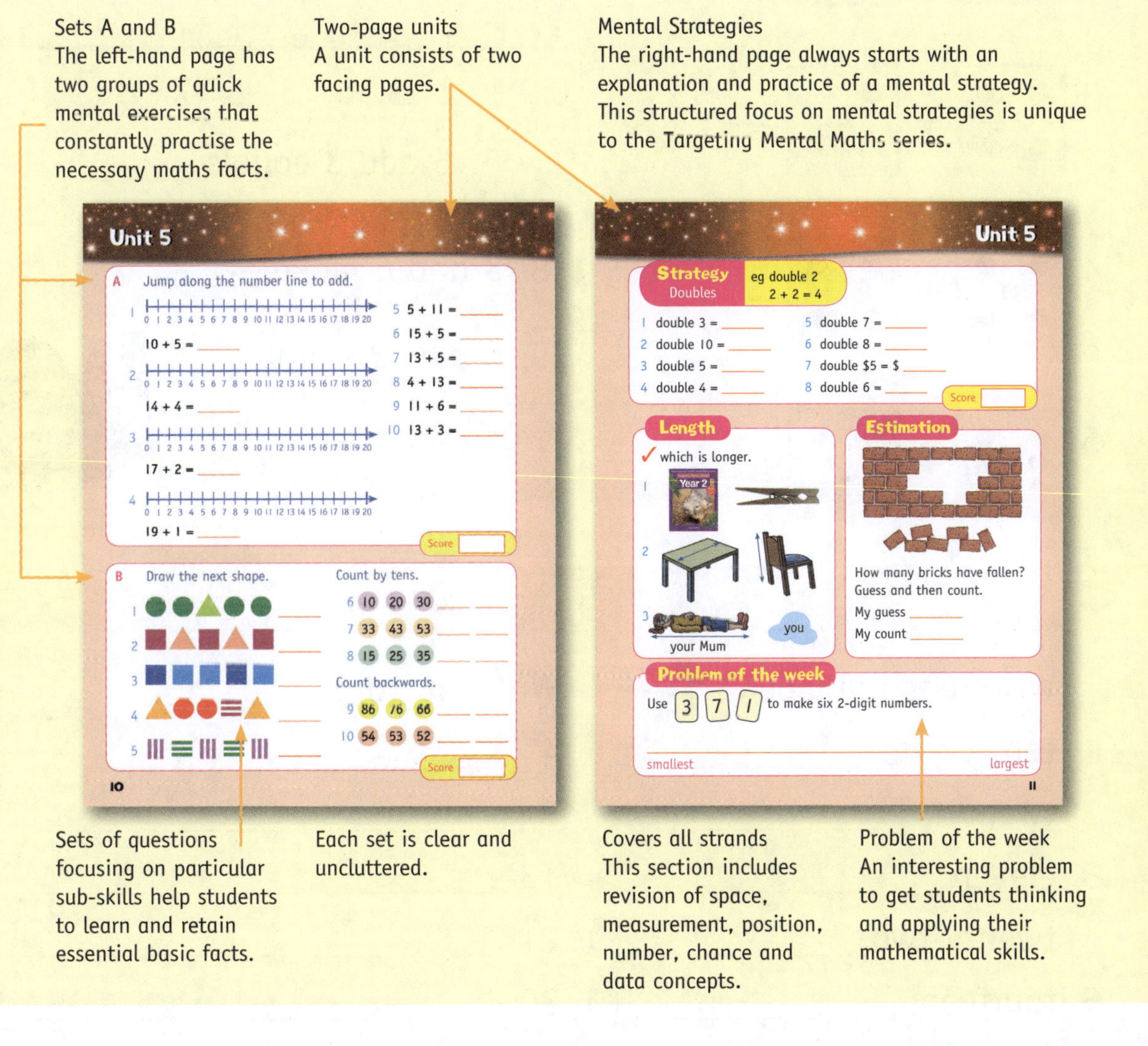

# Unit 1

**A** Add. Write the number.

1 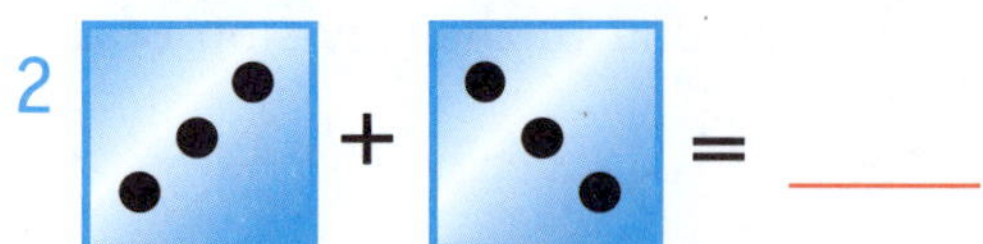 = ____

2  = ____

3 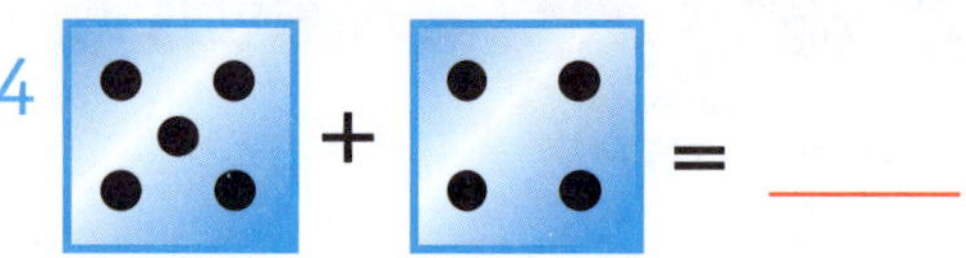 = ____

4 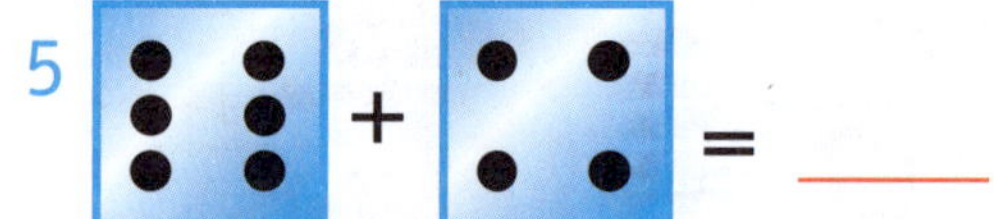 = ____

5 + = ____

6 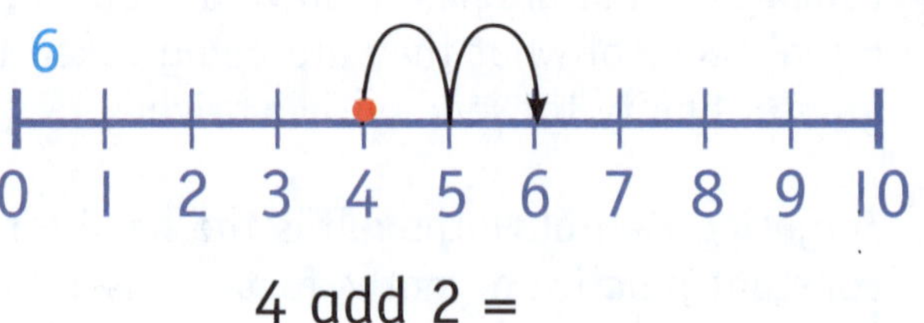


4 add 2 = ____

7 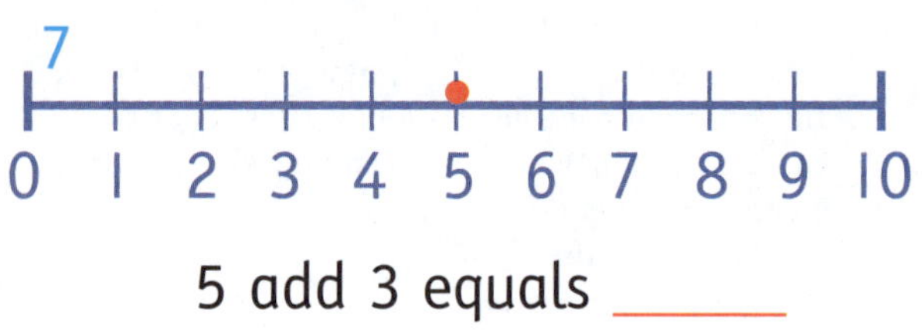


5 add 3 equals ____

8 3 and 6 make ____

9 6 plus 2 equals ____

10 4 and 4 is ____

Score

**B** Write each number.

1 ten ____

2 twenty ____

3 eleven ____

4 twenty-two ____

5 fourteen ____

Write in words.

6 4 ____

7 8 ____

8 13 ____

9 21 ____

10 30 ____

Score

**Strategy**
Using a number line

eg 2 + 3 = 5

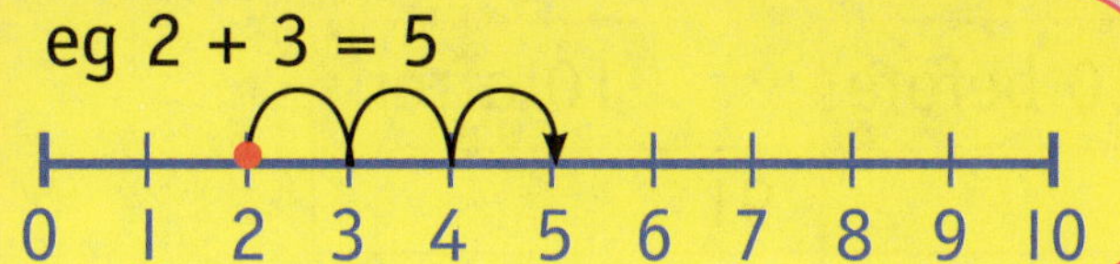

1 3 + 2 = ____

2 8 + 1 = ____

3 7 + 1 = ____

4 5 + 3 = ____

5 1 + 4 = ____

6 1 + 6 = ____

7 5 + 4 = ____

8 10 + 2 = ____

Score

How many groups of 2?

1

____ groups of 2 ____

2

____ groups of 2 = ____

3

____ groups of 2 = ____

Score

Count on.

1 4 + 2 = ____

2 5 + 1 = ____

3 6 + 4 = ____

4 8 + 1 = ____

5 7 + 4 = ____

Complete.

6 12 = ____ + ____

7 15 = ____ + ____

8 13 = ____ + ____

9 20 = ____ + ____

10 17 = ____ + ____

Score

# Unit 2

**A**

| | 10 before | | 10 after |
|---|---|---|---|
| 1 | | 91 | |
| 2 | | 24 | |
| 3 | | 66 | |
| 4 | | 55 | |
| 5 | | 80 | |

| | | between | |
|---|---|---|---|
| 6 | 20 | | 22 |
| 7 | 48 | | 50 |
| 8 | 36 | | 38 |
| 9 | 98 | | 100 |
| 10 | 58 | | 60 |

Score

**B** Count in 2s. How many eyes? ________

Score

**C** Circle the smaller number.

1 76, 90

2 80, 67

3 100, 20

Circle the larger number.

4 27, 26

5 36, 78

6 81, 19

Write each number.

7 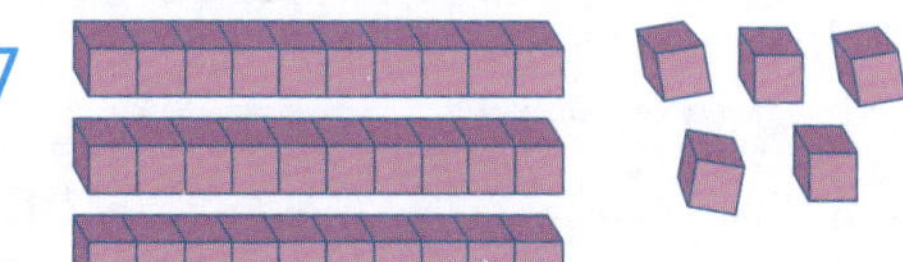 ________

8 ninety-nine ________

9 fifty ________

10 seventy-three ________

11 eighty ________

12 one hundred ________

Score

## Strategy
Counting on

6 + 2 = (6, 7, 8) = 8
8 + 3 = (8, 9, 10, 11) = 11

1 5 + 2 = ______

2 7 + 3 = ______

3 9 + 2 = ______

4 8 + 4 = ______

5 11 + 2 = ______

6 13 + 3 = ______

7 17 + 2 = ______

8 19 + 3 = ______

Score

## Space

Label each shape.

1

2

3

| Name | Number of sides | Number of corners |
|---|---|---|
| rectangle | | |
| triangle | | |
| pentagon | | |

4

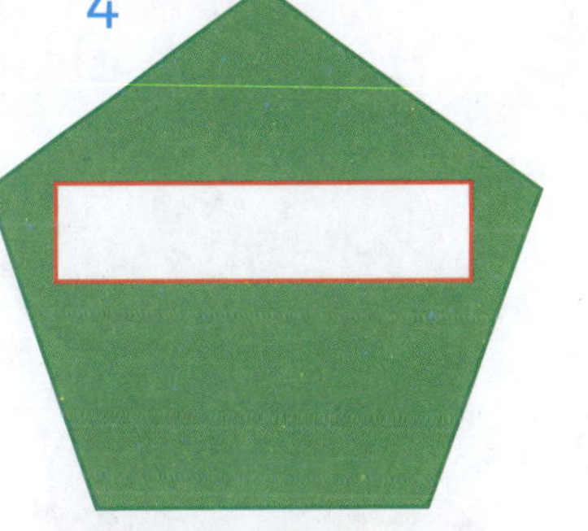

## Problem of the week

Adrian jumped in 5 puddles.

Jarrah jumped in 4 more puddles than Adrian.

How many puddles did Jarrah jump in? ______

**A**

| 1 less than: | | 10 more than: | | 10 less than: | |
|---|---|---|---|---|---|
| 1 | 40 ______ | 6 | 20 ______ | 11 | 80 ______ |
| 2 | 78 ______ | 7 | 50 ______ | 12 | 30 ______ |
| 3 | 14 ______ | 8 | 6 ______ | 13 | 71 ______ |
| 4 | 51 ______ | 9 | 56 ______ | 14 | 20 ______ |
| 5 | 99 ______ | 10 | 15 ______ | 15 | 96 ______ |

Score

**B** Complete.

74 73 ◯ ◯ 70 ◯ ◯ ◯ ◯ 65

Score

**C** How much altogether?

1  ______ c

2   ______ c

3  ______ c

4  = ______ c

5 30c + 10c = ______ c

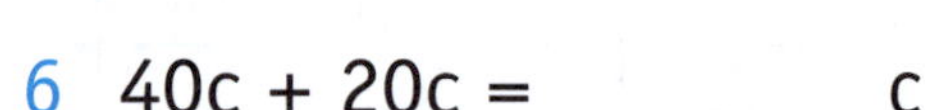

6 40c + 20c = ______ c

7 50c + 10c = ______ c

8 60c + 20c = ______ c

9 70c + 20c = ______ c

10 80c + 20c = ______ c

Score

# Unit 3

## Strategy
Counting in tens

1 20 + 10 = ______

2 10 + 30 = ______

3 80 + 10 = ______

4 50 + 10 = ______

5 60 + 30 = ______

6 40 + 40 = ______

7 40 + 20 = ______

8 70 + 20 = ______

Score

## Space

How many?

1

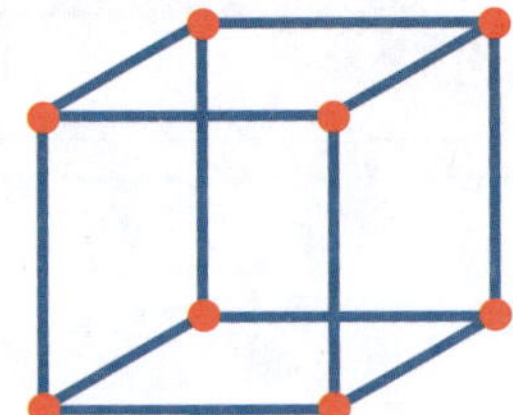

corners ______

edges ______

faces ______

2

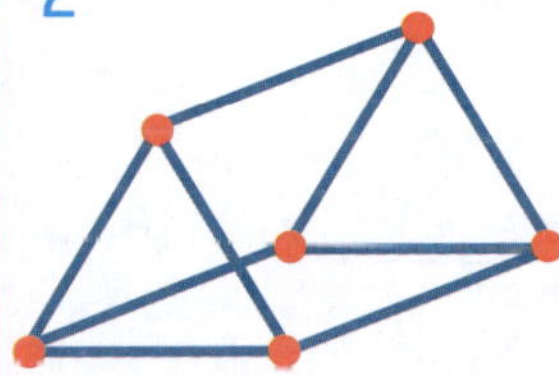

corners ______

edges ______

faces ______

## Symmetry

Colour to make a symmetrical pattern.

1

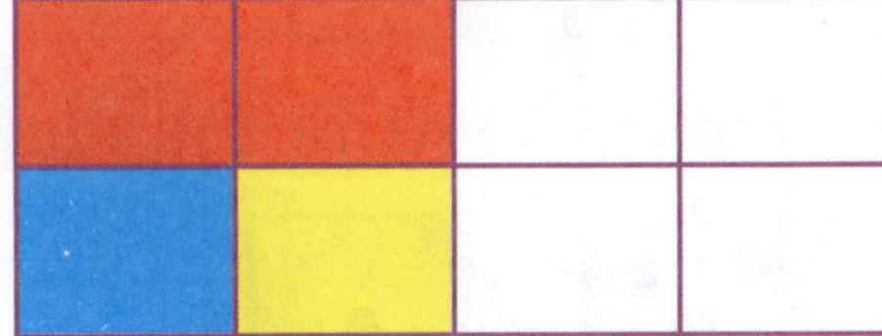

2

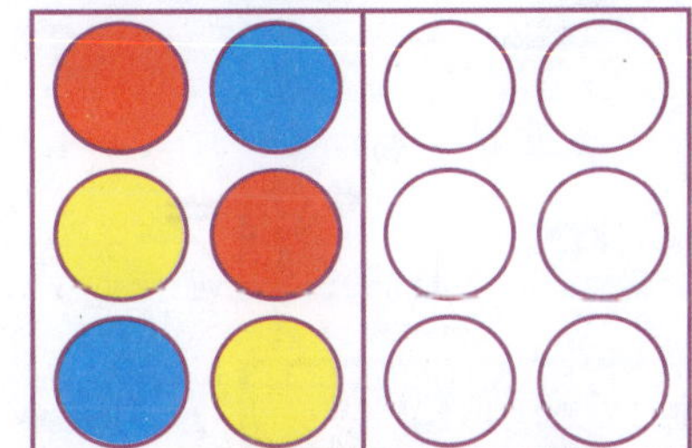

## Problem of the week

How old? Ash is 2 years older than Jack.
Jack is 4 years younger than Peta.
Peta is 10 years old.

Jack is ______ years old. Ash is ______ years old.

# Unit 4

**A** How many more to make ten?

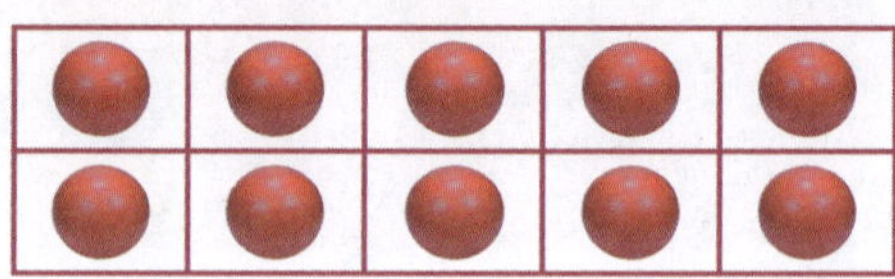

1 ______

2 ______

3 ______

4 ______

5 5 + ______ = 10

6 3 + ______ = 10

7 8 + ______ = 10

8 7 + ______ = 10

9 2 + ______ = 10

10 0 + ______ = 10

Score

**B** Subtract. Write the number.

1 − = ______

2 − = ______

3 − = ______

4 − = ______

5 − = ______

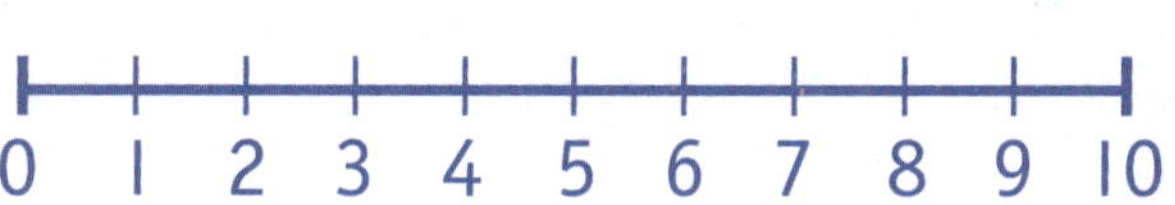


6 10 − 2 = ______

7 8 − 4 = ______

8 10 − 9 = ______

9 7 − 5 = ______

10 8 − 6 = ______

Score

## Strategy

### Odds and evens

Odds end in
1, 3, 5, 7, 9

Evens end in
0, 2, 4, 6, 8

Write the next odd number.

1 3, 5, 7, ______

2 9, 11, 13, ______

3 17, 19, 21, ______

4 35, 37, 39, ______

Write the next even number.

5 4, 6, 8, ______

6 22, 24, 26, ______

7 48, 50, 52, ______

8 66, 68, 70, ______

Score

## Space

Flip

Slide

Turn

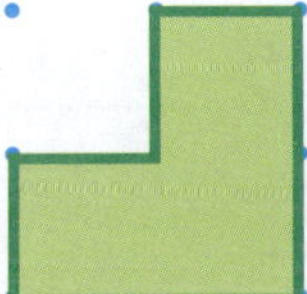

## Time

May

| S | M | T | W | T | F | S |
|---|---|---|---|---|---|---|
| | | | | 1 | 2 | 3 |
| 4 | 5 | 6 | 7 | 8 | 9 | 10 |
| 11 | 12 | 13 | 14 | 15 | 16 | 17 |
| 18 | 19 | 20 | 21 | 22 | 23 | 24 |
| 25 | 26 | 27 | 28 | 29 | 30 | 31 |

What day in May is:

2nd? ______

11th? ______

21st? ______

30th? ______

## Problem of the week

Paul added two odd numbers to get the answer 8.

What numbers did he use?

______ ______

Can you add two odd numbers and get an odd number? Why?

______

______

# Unit 5

**A** Jump along the number line to add.

1 

10 + 5 = ______

2 0 1 2 3 4 5 6 7 8 9 10 11 12 13 14 15 16 17 18 19 20

14 + 4 = ______

3 0 1 2 3 4 5 6 7 8 9 10 11 12 13 14 15 16 17 18 19 20

17 + 2 = ______

4 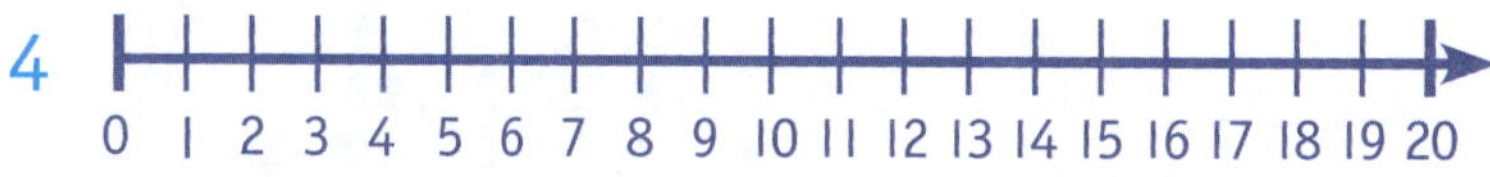

19 + 1 = ______

5 5 + 11 = ______ 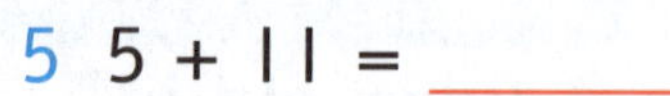

6 15 + 5 = ______

7 13 + 5 = ______

8 4 + 13 = ______

9 11 + 6 = ______

10 13 + 3 = ______

Score

**B** Draw the next shape.

1 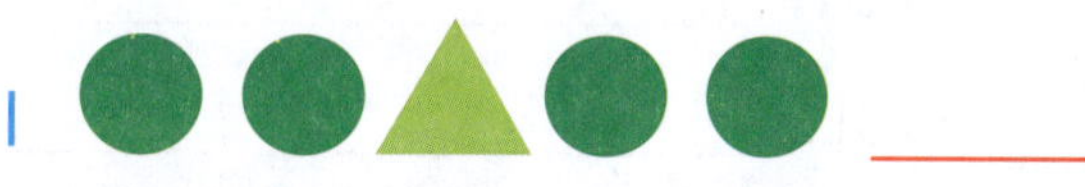 ______

2  ______

3  ______

4 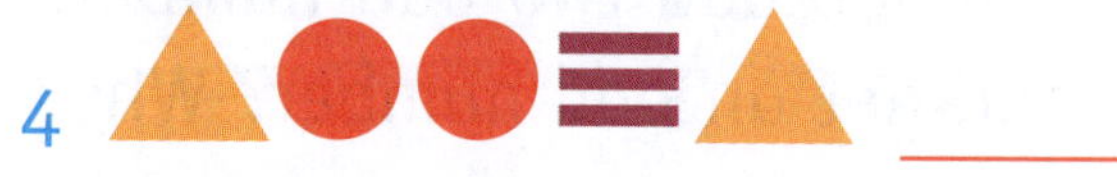 ______

5 ______

Count by tens.

6 10 20 30 ______ ______

7 33 43 53 ______ ______

8 15 25 35 ______ ______

Count backwards.

9 86 76 66 ______ ______

10 54 53 52 ______ ______

Score

# Unit 5

## Strategy
Doubles

eg double 2
2 + 2 = 4

1 double 3 = ______

2 double 10 = ______

3 double 5 = ______

4 double 4 = ______

5 double 7 = ______

6 double 8 = ______

7 double $5 = $ ______

8 double 6 = ______

Score

## Length

✓ which is longer.

1

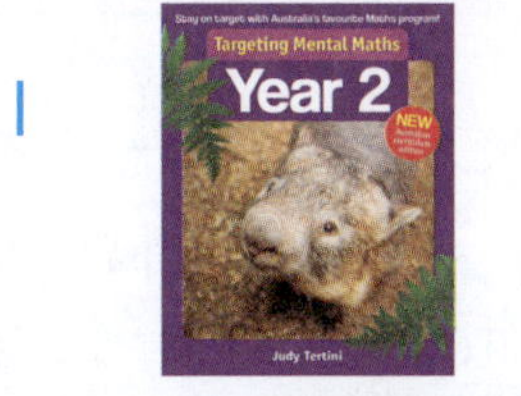


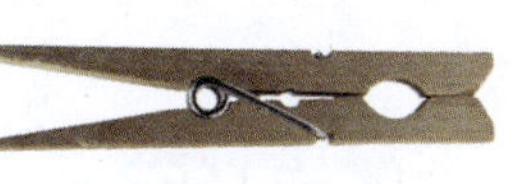

2

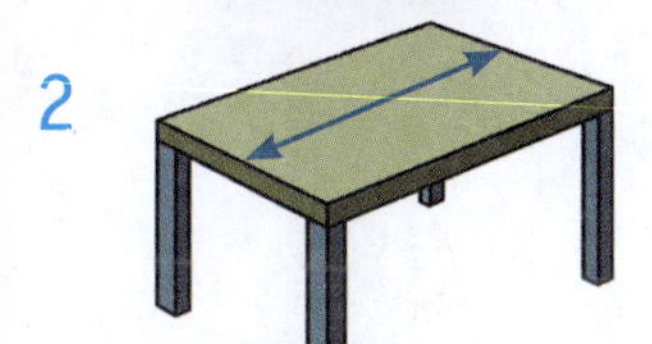

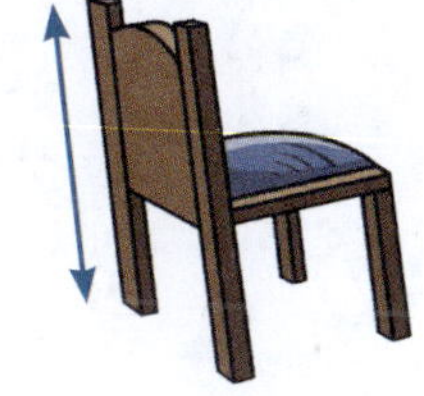

3

your Mum

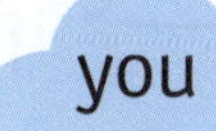


## Estimation

How many bricks have fallen?
Guess and then count.

My guess ______

My count ______

## Problem of the week

Use   1 to make six 2-digit numbers.

______________________________

smallest largest

# Unit 6

**A** How much for both?

1 $10 $2 = $ ______

2 $10 $4 = $ ______

3 $8 $8 = $ ______

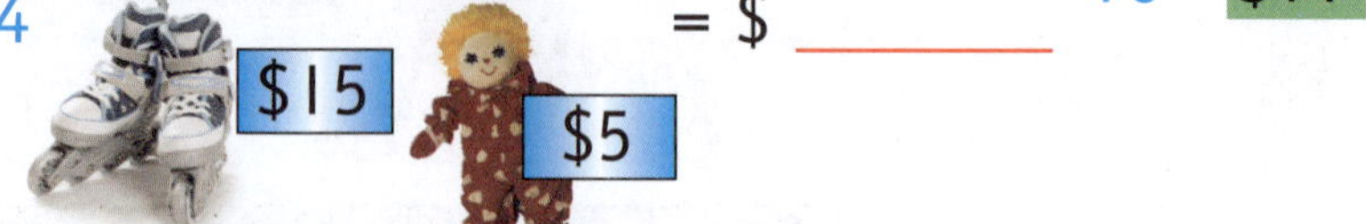

4 $15 $5 = $ ______

5 $19 $1 = $ ______

6 $14 $2 = $ ______

7 $12 $3 = $ ______

8 $10 $5 = $ ______

9 $2 $16 = $ ______

10 $11 $9 = $ ______

Score

## Time

**B** What is the time?

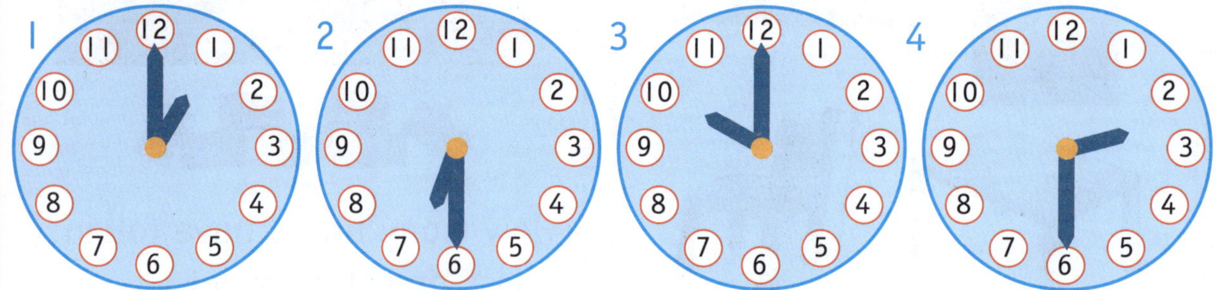

1 ____ o'clock

2 half-past ____

3 ____ o'clock

4 half-past ____

Write the digital times.

5 :

6 :

7 :

8 :

## Problem of the week

How many legs altogether? ______

## Strategy

Looking for tens

eg $3 + 1 + 7 = 10 + 1$
$= 11$

(10 marked above 3 + 7)

1 4 + 6 + 1 = ______

2 2 + 8 + 3 = ______

3 7 + 3 + 4 = ______

4 9 + 1 + 5 = ______

5 10 + 0 + 8 = ______

6 1 + 7 + 9 = ______

7 3 + 6 + 7 = ______

8 1 + 8 + 9 = ______

Score

## Mass

Circle the heavier one.

1

2

## Half

Draw a line to cut into halves.

1

2

3

4

## Problem of the week

What could you buy with $1 and have no change?

______

# Unit 7

**A** How much?

1 

2 

3  

4 

5 

6 

Score

    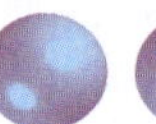  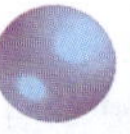 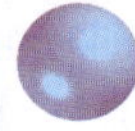 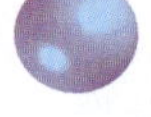

**B**

1 $8 - 3 =$ ______

2 $10 - 2 =$ ______

3 $7 - 4 =$ ______

4 $9 - 2 =$ ______

5 $10 - 7 =$ ______

6 $10 - 5 =$ ______

7 $10 - 10 =$ ______

8 $8 - 6 =$ ______

9 $9 - 5 =$ ______

10 $10 - 8 =$ ______

Score

**C** How many?

1 days in a week ______

2 hours in a day ______

3 minutes in an hour ______

4 months in a year ______

5 years in a decade ______

Write the ordinal number.

6 first ______

7 third ______

8 sixth ______

9 eighth ______

10 fourth ______

Score

## Strategy
Counting back

9 − 2 = (9, 8, 7) = 7
8 − 3 = (8, 7, 6, 5) = 5

1 6 − 2 = ______
2 8 − 5 = ______
3 9 − 4 = ______
4 10 − 3 = ______
5 12 − 2 = ______
6 16 − 3 = ______
7 19 − 2 = ______
8 18 − 3 = ______

Score

## Fractions

Colour to match the label.

1
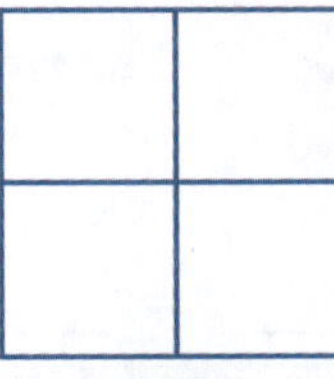
$\frac{1}{2}$

2
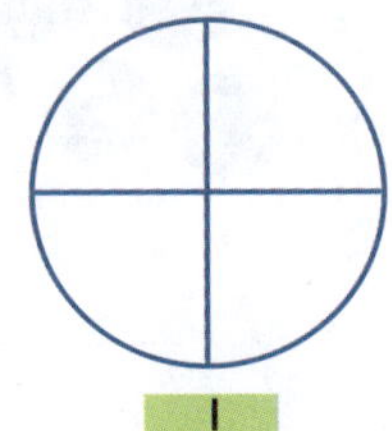
$\frac{1}{2}$

Circle the fraction.

3
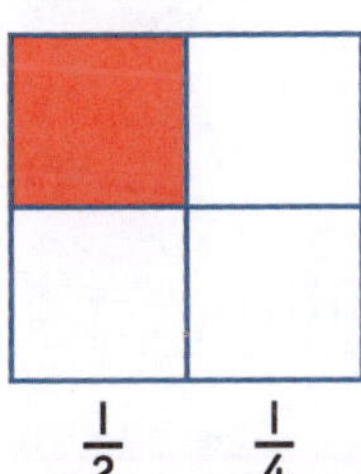
$\frac{1}{2}$ $\frac{1}{4}$

4
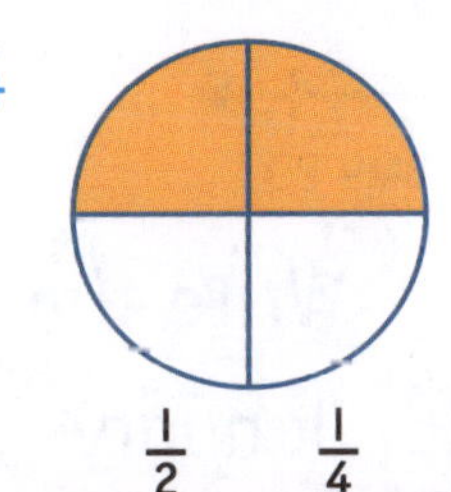
$\frac{1}{2}$ $\frac{1}{4}$

## Calculators

Press 2 + + =

Now press = = = = =

Write each number.

Press C

Press 3 + + =

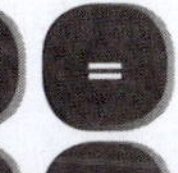

Now press = = = = =

## Problem of the week

What score did Ben get?

______

**A** Count forward:

1 by ones.

56, 57, ____, ____, ____

2 by tens.

31, 41, ____, ____, ____

Count backwards:

3 by ones.

77, 76, ____, ____, ____

4 by tens.

80, 70, ____, ____, ____

Order from smallest to largest.

5 80, 15, 75, 57, 50

____, ____, ____, ____, ____

6 Colour the ones that match.

| 2 + 3 | | 4 + 1 |
|---|---|---|
| | 5 | |
| 3 + 3 | | 2 + 2 |

7

| before | | after |
|---|---|---|
| | 24 | |
| | 40 | |
| | 15 | |

8 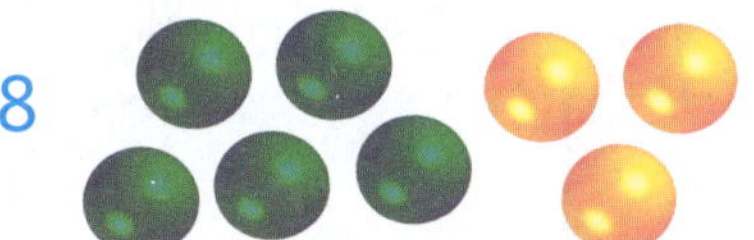

____ + ____ = ____

Score

0 1 2 3 4 5 6 7 8 9 10 11 12 13 14 15 16 17 18 19 20

**C** Use the number line to help.

1 6 + 5 = ____

2 14 + 2 = ____

3 $17 + $3 = $ ____

4 7 − 1 = ____

5 10 − 2 = ____

Write the season.

6 January ____

7 June ____

How many?

8 days in a week ____

9 months in a year ____

10 months in a season ____

Score

## Strategy

Use the strategies you have learnt.

1 9 + 2 = ____
2 19 + 3 = ____
3 9 – 4 = ____
4 10 – 3 = ____
5 double 5 = ____
6 double 3 = ____
7 The next even number. 48, 50, 52, ____
8 The next odd number. 9, 11, 13, ____
9 3 + 6 + 7 = ____
10 2 + 1 + 8 = ____

Score

## Space

Match.

pentagon

triangle

circle

hexagon

## Fractions

1 Colour one half ($\frac{1}{2}$).

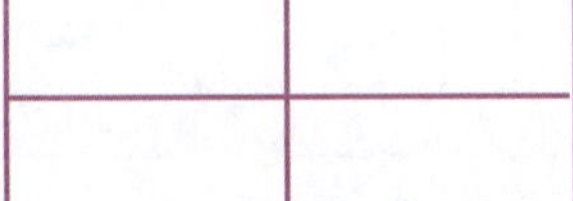

2 Colour one quarter ($\frac{1}{4}$).

## Time

What time is it?

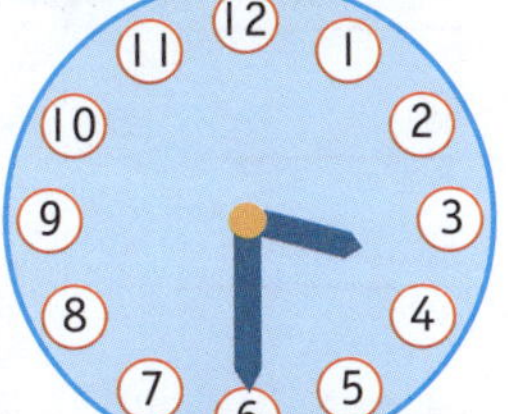

1 half-past ____

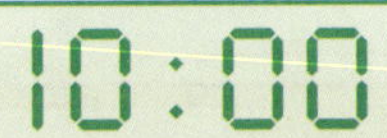


2 ____ o'clock

## Mass

Draw something heavier.

# Unit 9

## A

| 3 | 4 |
|---|---|
| 7 | |

1. 3 + 4 = [_]
2. 4 + [_] = [_]

| 5 | 4 |
|---|---|
| 9 | |

3. 5 + [_] = [_]
4. 4 + [_] = [_]

| 3 | 5 |
|---|---|
| 8 | |

5. [_] + [_] = [_]
6. [_] + [_] = [_]

Score

## B Order.

91 68 86 78

smallest largest

Score

## C Write P (possible) or I (impossible).

**Today**

1 It will snow. ______
2 You will turn 100. ______
3 You will read. ______
4 You will eat. ______
5 You will watch T.V. ______

$1 less.

6 $100 $______
7 $49 $______
8 $15 $______
9 $85 $______
10 $1000 $______

Score

## Strategy

Counting back using a number line

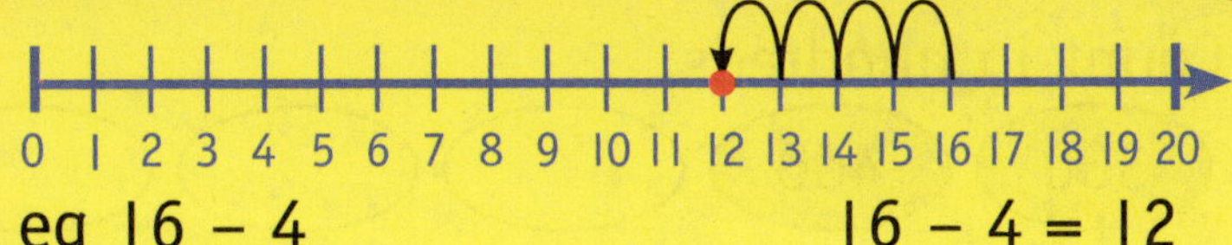


eg 16 – 4

16 – 4 = 12

1 8 – 2 = ______

2 10 – 6 = ______

3 12 – 3 = ______

4 14 – 4 = ______

5 18 – 4 = ______

6 16 – 5 = ______

7 19 – 3 = ______

8 20 – 9 = ______

Score

## Capacity

Tick the one that holds the most.

2

## 2D shapes

Colour the circles.

## Problem of the week

Audrey planted 3 rows of carrots. She planted 4 carrots in each row. Snails ate 5 carrots. How many were left? ______

# Unit 10

**A** Count in hundreds.

1  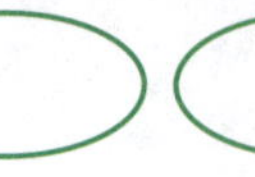  

300, 400, ____, ____, ____, ____, ____

Write the number 100 more than:

2 300 ______

3 100 ______

4 700 ______

5 900 ______

Write the number 100 less than:

7 300 ______

8 100 ______

9 500 ______

10 900 ______

How much?

6    

$ ______

Score ______

**B** 

How many more to make ten?

1 8 + ______ = 10

2 6 + ______ = 10

3 5 + ______ = 10

4 7 + ______ = 10

5 3 + ______ = 10

How many fingers?

6  ______

7  ______

8  ______

9 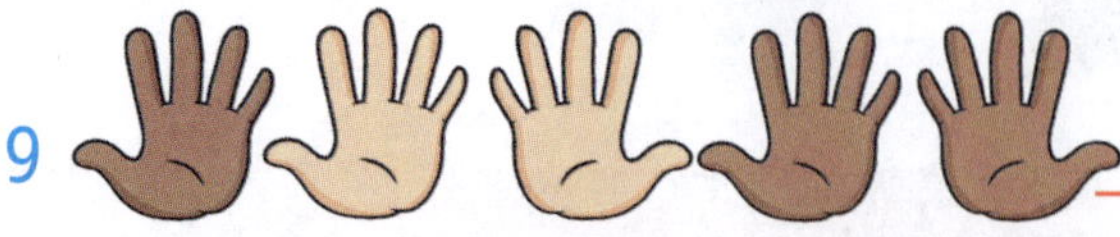 ______

10 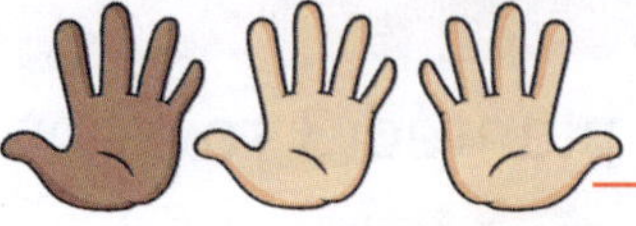 ______

Score ______

## Strategy
Counting on

Count on to find the difference.
eg 20 − 16 = (16, 17, 18, 19, 20) = 4
38 − 34 = (34, 35, 36, 37, 38) = 4

1 30 − 26 = ______
2 48 − 45 = ______
3 56 − 52 = ______
4 84 − 80 = ______
5 77 − 74 = ______
6 92 − 89 = ______
7 100 − 96 = ______
8 400 − 397 = ______

Score

## Money

Draw one coin to match.

1  =

2  =

## Space

Draw. 

1 front view 

2 top view

3 side view

## Problem of the week

Peter has 4 fish bowls.
There are 3 fish in each bowl.

How many fish altogether? ______

How much if each fish cost 20c? ______

**A** 0 1 2 3 4 5 6 7 8 9 10 11 12 13 14 15 16 17 18 19 20

How many more to make 20?

1  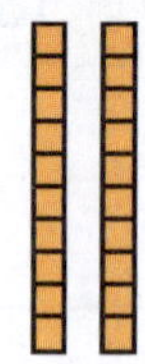

_____ + _____ = 20

2 9 + ☐ = 20

3 5 + ☐ = 20

4 13 + ☐ = 20

5 ☐ + 8 = 20

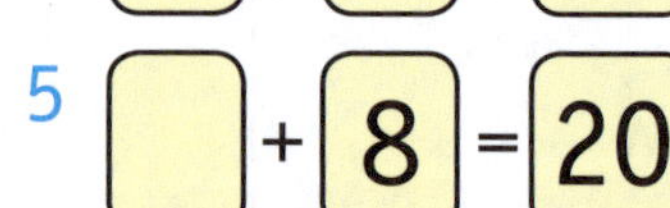

How much more to make $20?

6  

7  

8   

9 

10  

Score

**B** Order from smallest to largest.

960 530 350 109

Score

**C** How much altogether?

1 50c + 50c = _____

2 20c + 50c = _____

3 10c + 5c = _____

4 20c + 20c = _____

5 $1 + 50c = _____

Write the school days in order.

6 ______________________

7 ______________________

8 ______________________

9 ______________________

10 ______________________

Score

## Strategy
Taking away ten

eg 70 – 10 = 60 Count back by 10s.

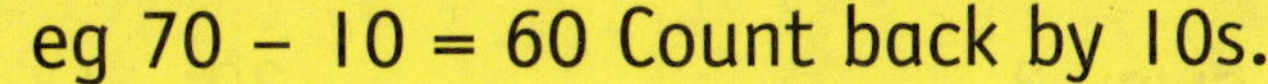


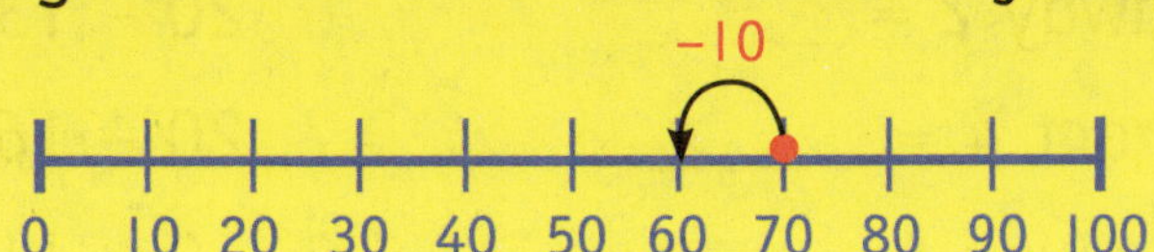


1 80 – 10 = ______

2 60 – 10 = ______

3 40 – 10 = ______

4 90 – 10 = ______

5 70 – 10 = ______

6 30 – 10 = ______

7 40 – 20 = ______

8 100 – 20 = ______

Score

## Turns

______ turn

______ turn

______ turn

______ turn

## Volume

Join shapes with the same volume.

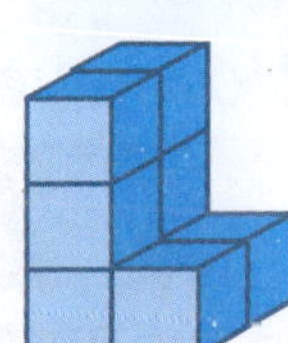

## Problem of the week

What is my number plate?
One digit is 20 – 13.
Another digit is 3 + 3 + 3.
The third digit is 10 + 4 - 6.
The digits are written from largest to smallest.

AAV ______ ______ ______

# Unit 12

**A**

1 8 take away 2 = ______
2 10 subtract 4 = ______
3 16 take away 4 = ______
4 19 subtract 6 = ______
5 17 take away 10 = ______
6 20 − 13 = ______
7 20 − 16 = ______
8 19 − 11 = ______
9 18 − 13 = ______
10 17 − 15 = ______

Score

**B** Find the change.

1 

$______ − $______ = $______

2 

$______ − $______ = $______

Score

**C** How much more to make $20?

1  ______

2 How much change from $20?

______

What is the new price?

3 25c 5c off ______ c
4 60c 10c off ______ c
5 $1 10c off ______ c

6 13 − 5 = ______
7 20 − 4 = ______
8 19 − 11 = ______

Count on to find the difference.

9 48 53 ______
10 33 41 ______

Score

## Strategy
### Subtracting teens

eg 20 – 14 = 6
Take away the 10 and then take away the ones.

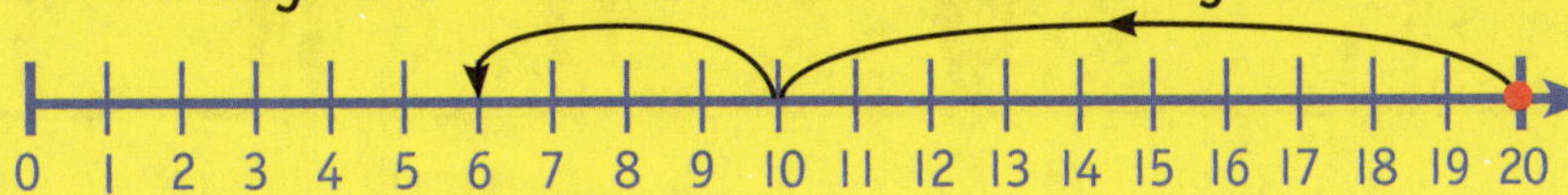


1 20 – 12 = ______

2 20 – 16 = ______

3 19 – 12 = ______

4 18 – 11 = ______

5 17 – 13 = ______

6 16 – 14 = ______

7 16 – 12 = ______

8 17 – 15 = ______

Score

## Position

| Tim | Tom | Sue |
| --- | --- | --- |
| Ben | Rick | Sam |
| Joe | Jan | Kim |

Who is:

1 below Tom? ______

2 above Joe? ______

3 to the left of Jan? ______

4 next to Kim? ______

5 between Tim and Sue? ______

## Calculators

Press  2  0  +  +  4  = 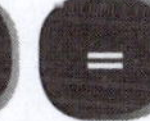 Now keep pressing  =

## Problem of the week

If 10 mangoes fill one box:

1 how many boxes will 50 mangoes fill? ______

2 how many mangoes in $3\frac{1}{2}$ boxes? ______

# Unit 13

**A** Count back 4 spaces from each number.

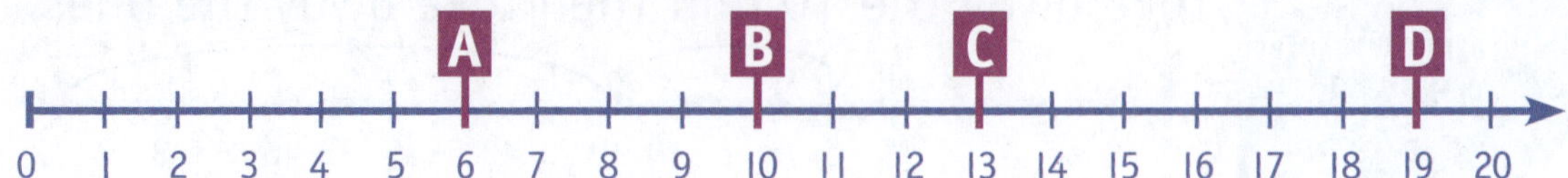


1 **A** = ______ 2 **B** = ______ 3 **C** = ______ 4 **D** = ______

Count on to find the difference.

5 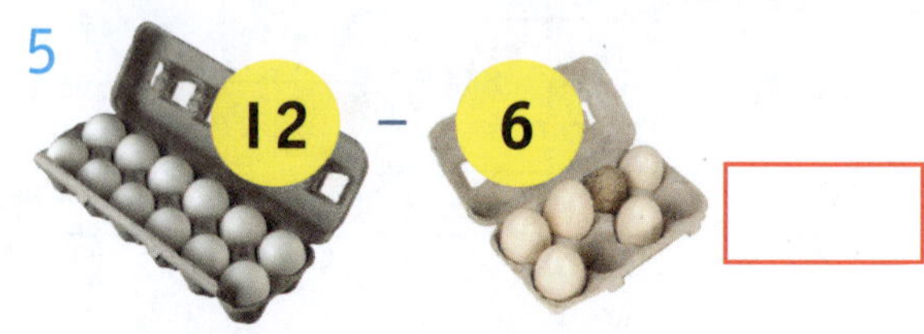


6 

7 

8 

52 – 48 = ______

9 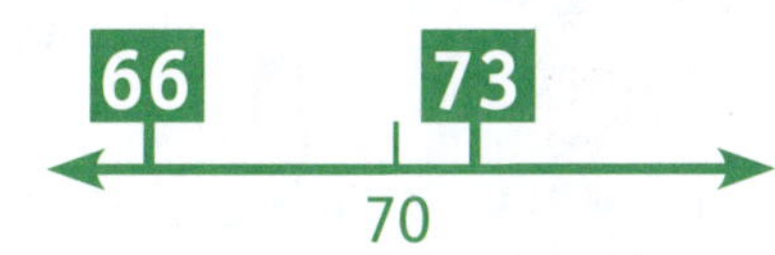


73 – 66 = ______

10 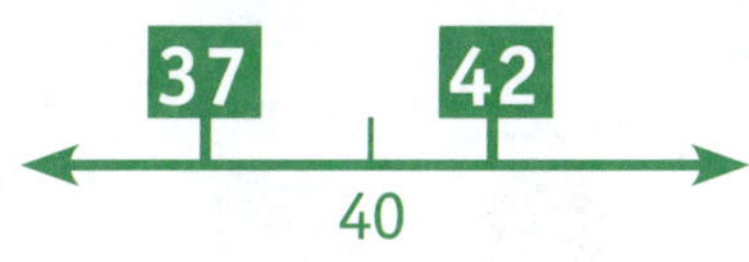


42 – 37 = ______

Score

**B** Circle the larger number.

1 215, 251

2 410, 456

3 777, 717

Circle the smaller number.

4 1000, 100

5 200, 199

How much change from $20?

6 $11 = ______

7 $5 = ______

8 $10 = ______

9 $12 = ______

10 $2 = ______

Score

## Strategy
Counting by fives

30, 35, 40, 45, 50 55, 50, 45, 40, 35

1 5, 10, 15, _____, _____

2 55, 60, 65, _____, _____

3 70, 75, 80, _____, _____

4 420, 425, 430, _____, _____

5 100, 95, 90 , _____, _____

6 640, 645, 650, _____

7 950, 955, 960, _____

8 = _____ c

Score

## Data

Which sport was:

1 most popular? _____

2 least popular? _____

## Time

Write the digital time.

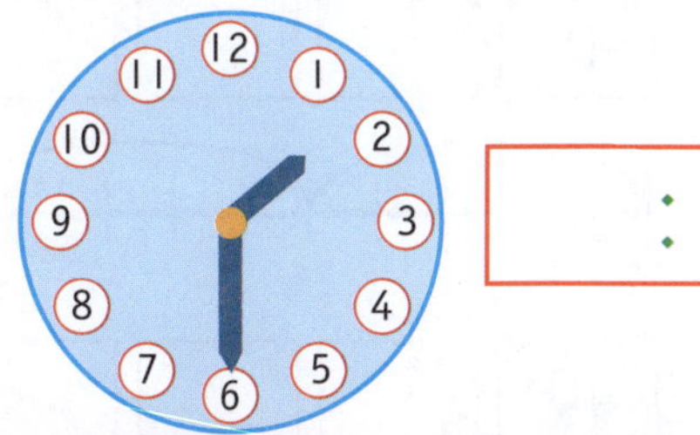

:

## Chance

unlikely or likely ?

You will find $100 today.

_____

## Problem of the week

On paper write two lists.

1 animals that are heavier than you

2 animals that are lighter than you

# Unit 14

**A**

1 3 + 6 = ______

2 4 + 3 = ______

3 8 + 2 = ______

4 6 + 3 = ______

5 5 + 5 = ______

6 9 − 2 = ______

7 8 − 6 = ______

8 10 − 5 = ______

9 9 − 3 = ______

10 9 − 1 = ______

Score

**B** Make equal jumps along the number line.
Write the numbers you land on.

1
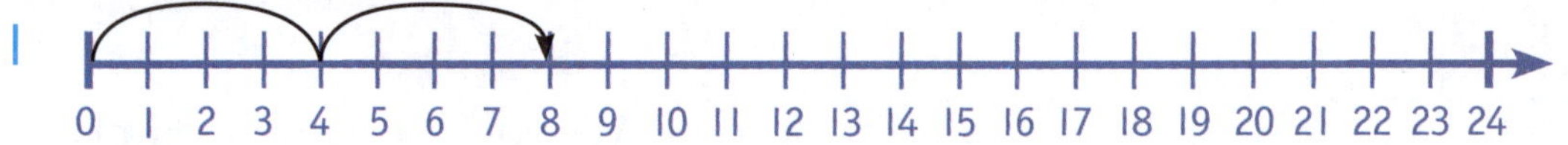

The rule is ______.

2
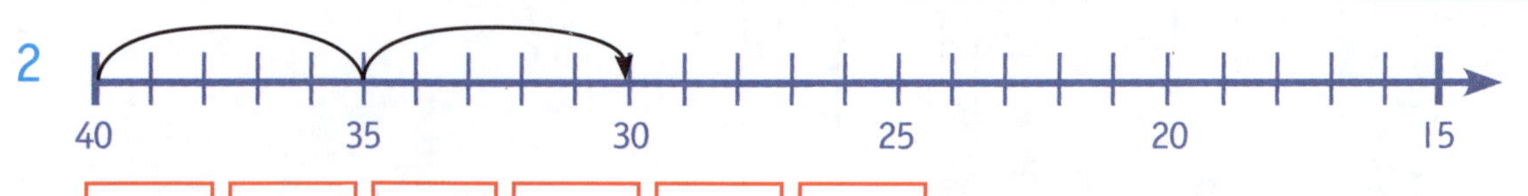

The rule is ______.

Continue each pattern.

3 3, 6, 9, ______, ______

4 20, 25, 30, ______, ______

Score

**C** Circle the even number.

1 10, 15

2 111, 168

3 596, 719

4 741, 742

5 104, 117

6 double 5 = ______

7 double 10 = ______

8 double 7 = ______

9 double \$2 = \$ ______

10 double \$6 = \$ ______

Score

## Strategy
Looking for patterns

eg 3 + 2 = 5
13 + 2 = 15
23 + 2 = 25

| 1 | | 2 | | 3 | |
|---|---|---|---|---|---|
| | 4 + 5 = ______ | | 8 + 1 = ______ | | 3 + 4 = ______ |
| | 14 + 5 = ______ | | 18 + 1 = ______ | | 13 + 4 = ______ |
| | 24 + 5 = ______ | | 28 + 1 = ______ | | 23 + 4 = ______ |
| | 44 + 5 = ______ | | 68 + 1 = ______ | | 53 + 4 = ______ |

Score

## Halves

1 Divide in half.

half of ______ is ______

2 Brendan had 10 masks.
He gave half of them away.
How many are left? ______

## Data

1 How many did Ian win? ______

2 How many did Peter win? ______

3 How many medals did the team win altogether? ______

## Problem of the week

Cathy has 20 T-shirts. Six are red. Eight are blue.
The rest are green. Three green ones are torn.
How many green T-shirts are left? ______

# Unit 15

**A** Count in fives.

| | | | | |
|---|---|---|---|---|
| 1 | 20 | 25 | 30 | ______ |
| 2 | 100 | 95 | 90 | ______ |
| 3 | 60 | 55 | 50 | ______ |
| 4 | 80 | 85 | 90 | ______ |

5 ______ c

Write the new price.

| | | | |
|---|---|---|---|
| 6 | 10c | 5c off | ______ c |
| 7 | 50c | 5c off | ______ c |
| 8 | 75c | 5c off | ______ c |
| 9 | 80c | 10c off | ______ c |
| 10 | $1 | 10c off | ______ c |

Score

**B** 1

3 + 3 + 3 = ______

______ threes are ______

2

4 + 4 + 4 + 4 = ______

______ fours are ______

Score

**C** Count on to find the difference.

| | | | |
|---|---|---|---|
| 1 | 13 | 18 | ______ |
| 2 | 24 | 31 | ______ |
| 3 | 58 | 63 | ______ |
| 4 | 63 | 66 | ______ |
| 5 | 83 | 87 | ______ |

How much?

6 10 + 10 = ______

7 10 + 10 + 10 + 10 + 10 = ______

8 10 + 10 + 10 = ______

9 10 + 10 + 10 + 10 + 10 + 10 = ______

10 10 + 10 + 10 + 10 = ______

Score

# Unit 15

## Strategy ×2

eg 4 × 2 = 8 is the same as 2 + 2 + 2 + 2 = 8

1 2 × 2 = ______

2 3 × 2 = ______

3 5 × 2 = ______

4 6 × 2 = ______

5 7 × 2 = ______

6 8 × 2 = ______

7 9 × 2 = ______

8 10 × 2 = ______

Score

## Space

Match.

sphere

cube

cone

cylinder

## Problem of the week

Sonia bought.

1 How much did she save? ______

2 She paid $1.70 for cereal. What is its normal price? ______

**A**

1 Continue the pattern.

0, 3, 6, ______, ______

What is the rule? ______

2 Count in 5s.

60, 55, 50, ______, ______

Count forwards:

3 78, 79, 80, ______, ______

4 70, 80, 90, ______, ______

5 390, 490, 590, ______, ______

6 100, 200, 300, ______, ______

How many?

7 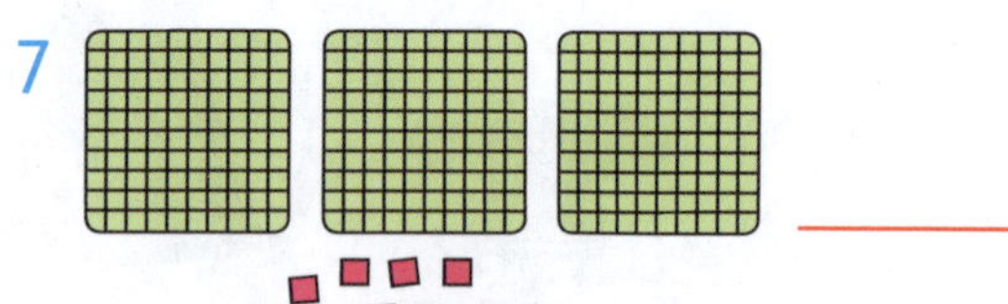 ______

8 

$3 + 3 =$ ______

2 threes are ______

9 

$4 + 4 + 4 =$ ______

3 fours are = ______

10

$\frac{1}{2}$ of 10 = ______

Score

**B**

1 $\frac{1}{2}$ of 20 = ______

2 $\frac{1}{2}$ of 10 = ______

3 $\frac{1}{2}$ of 8 = ______

4 $\frac{1}{2}$ of 16 = ______

5 $\frac{1}{2}$ of 4 = ______

6 $3 \times 10c =$ ______ c

7 $5 \times 10c =$ ______ c

8 $6 \times 10c =$ ______ c

9 $8 \times 10c =$ ______ c

10 $10 \times 10c =$ ______ c

Score

## Strategy

Use strategies you have learnt.

1 17 − 12 = ______
2 18 − 11 = ______
3 4 + 5 = ______
4 14 + 5 = ______
5 5, 10, 15, ______, ______
6 30 − 26 = ______
7 100 − 96 = ______
8 2 × 2 = ______
9 16 − 4 = ______
10 19 − 3 = ______

Score

## Fractions

Colour one 8th.

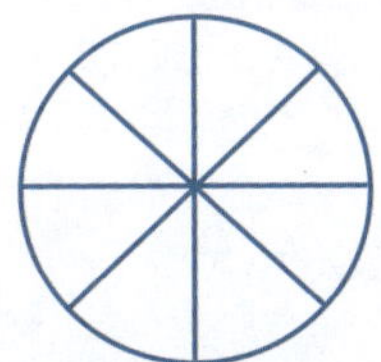

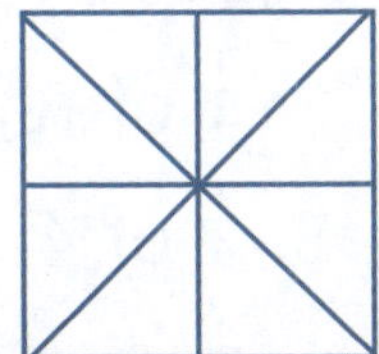

## Symmetry

Draw the line of symmetry.

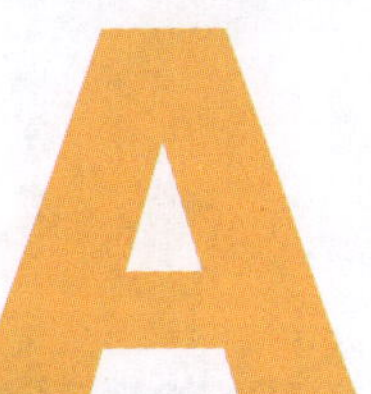


## Data

| Colour | Tally | Total |
|---|---|---|
| yellow | | |
| red | | |

## Chance

Write something that is certain to happen.

______
______
______

## Time

Draw the analogue time.

1 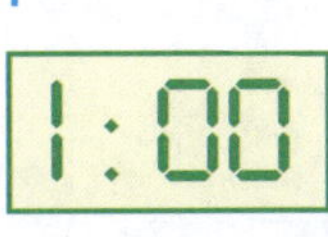


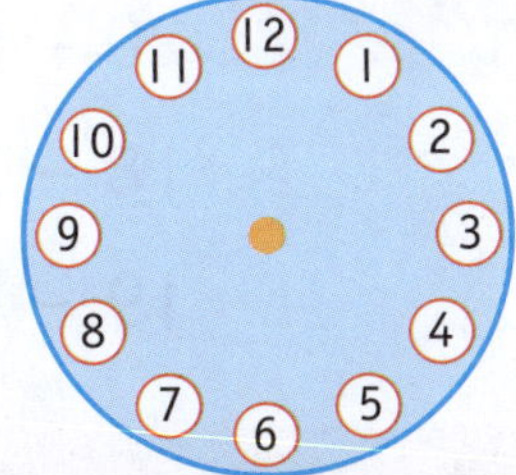


2 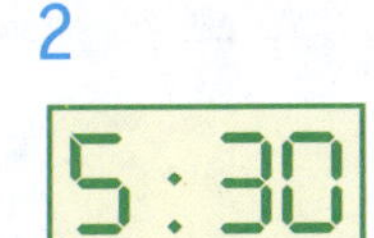

# Unit 17

**A**

| 2 | 3 |
|---|---|
| 5 | |

1. 5 - 2 = [_]
2. 5 - 3 = [_]

| 2 | 4 |
|---|---|
| 6 | |

3. 6 - 2 = [_]
4. 6 - [_] = [_]

| 2 | 5 |
|---|---|
| 7 | |

5. 7 - [_] = [_]
6. [_] - [_] = [_]

Score

**B** 1

one quarter of _____ is _____

2 $\frac{1}{4}$ of 8 = _____

3 $\frac{1}{4}$ of 4 = _____

4 $\frac{1}{4}$ of 12 = _____

Score

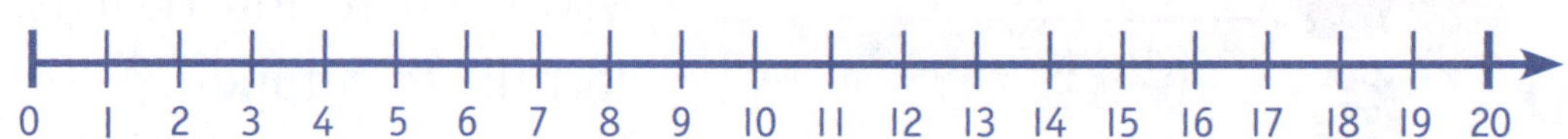


**C** Add.

1 15 + 5 = _____

2 12 + 3 = _____

3 16 + 4 = _____

4 18 + 1 = _____

5 11 + 9 = _____

Subtract.

6 15 – 5 = _____

7 14 – 3 = _____

8 20 – 5 = _____

9 18 – 3 = _____

10 19 – 6 = _____

Score

## Strategy
10 more than

Add one to the tens digit.
eg 10 more than 17
17 + 10 = 27

1 15 + 10 = ________
2 10 + 10 = ________
3 11 + 10 = ________
4 14 + 10 = ________
5 18 + 10 = ________
6 25 + 10 = ________
7 73 + 10 = ________
8 80 + 10 = ________

Score

## Fractions

Colour $\frac{1}{4}$ red, $\frac{1}{4}$ blue, $\frac{1}{2}$ green.

1 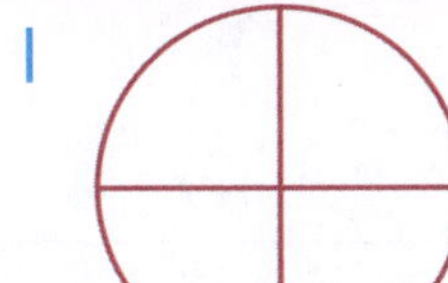

2 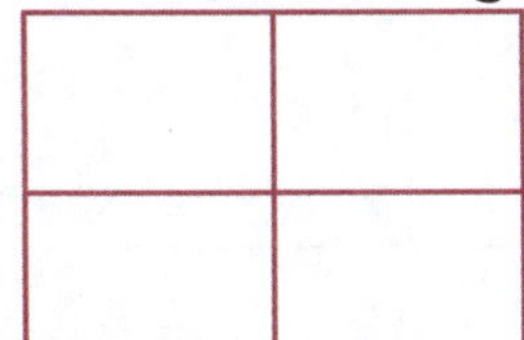

3 

## Time

June 2005

| S | M | T | W | T | F | S |
|---|---|---|---|---|---|---|
| | | | 1 | 2 | 3 | 4 |
| 5 | 6 | 7 | 8 | 9 | 10 | 11 |
| 12 | 13 | 14 | 15 | 16 | 17 | 18 |
| 19 | 20 | 21 | 22 | 23 | 24 | 25 |
| 26 | 27 | 28 | 29 | 30 | | |

How many:

1 days in June? ________
2 Mondays in June? ________
3 Circle 7th June and 26th June.

## Problem of the week

Megan began reading at 5 o'clock and read for $4\frac{1}{2}$ hours.
Rose began reading at 4 o'clock and read for 6 hours.

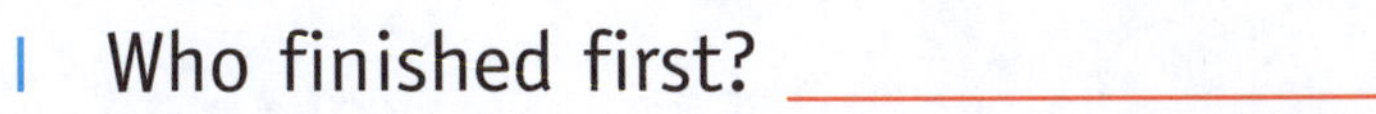

1 Who finished first? ________
2 What time did she finish reading? ________

# Unit 18

**A** Write in numerals.

1 three hundred and fifty-six ______

2 six hundred and twenty-one ______

3 four hundred and thirteen ______

4 nine hundred and ten ______

Complete.

5 219 = ______ + ______ + ______

6 687 = ______ + ______ + ______

7 140 = ______ + ______ + ______

Write in words.

8 568 ______

9 996 ______

How many?

10

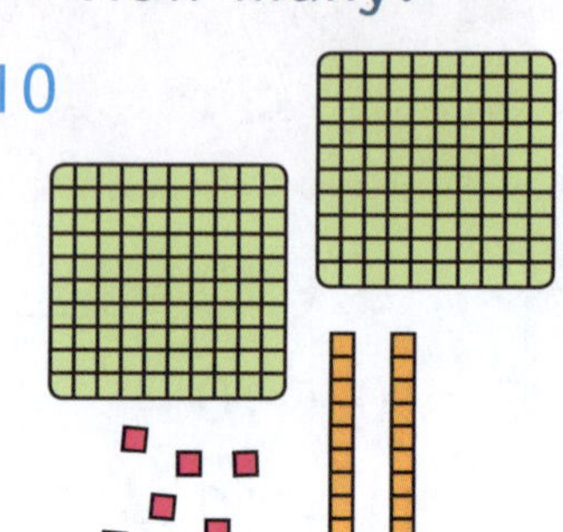

______

Score

**B** Circle the odd number.

1 61, 108

2 24, 107

3 36, 703

4 905, 410

5 899, 900

Circle the larger number.

6 109, 190

7 301, 299

8 648, 569

9 885, 929

10 250, 502

Score

**C** Find $\frac{1}{4}$.

1 20 ______ 2 12 ______ 3 16 ______ 4 40 ______

Score

## Strategy ×10

Add a 0.
eg 2 × 10 = 20
3 × 10 = 30

1 4 × 10 = ______

2 6 × 10 = ______

3 5 × 10 = ______

4 10 × 10 = ______

5 3 × 10c = ______ c

6 8 × 10c = ______ c

7 9 × 10c = ______ c

8 10 × 10c = ______ c

Score

## Flip, slide, turn

Match.

flip slide turn

1 

2 

3 

## Time

Draw and write the time. I started reading at 3 o'clock and finished at half-past four.

start: 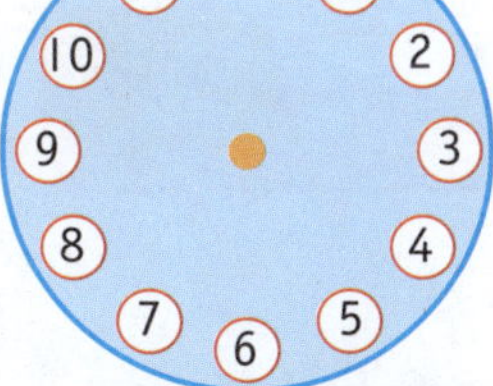

:

finish: 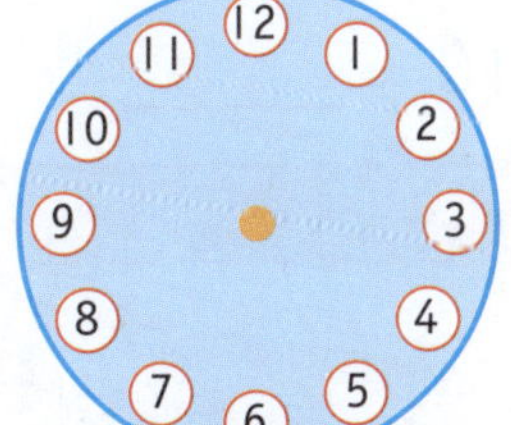

:

## Problem of the week

There are 20 cars.

$\frac{1}{2}$ are red, $\frac{1}{4}$ are blue, 1 is yellow. The rest are green.

How many are red? ______ blue? ______ green? ______

# Unit 19

**A** Count forwards.

1 41, 42, 43, ______, ______

2 10, 20, 30, ______, ______

3 300, 400, 500, ______, ______

Count backwards.

4 50, 49, 48, ______, ______

5 700, 600, 500, ______, ______

6 86, 76, 66, ______, ______

How many?

7 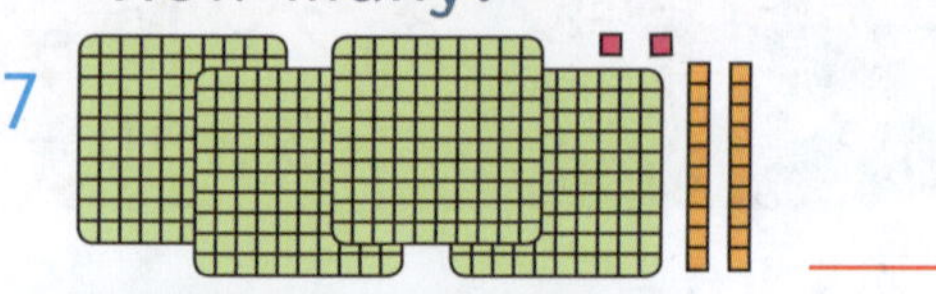 ______

8 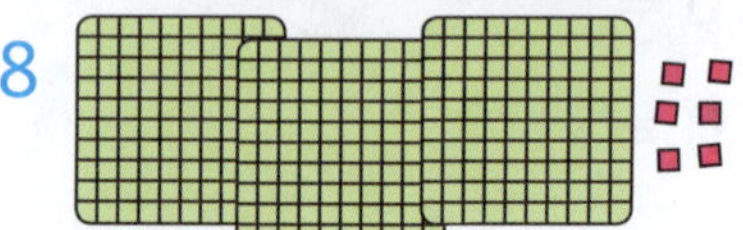 ______

9 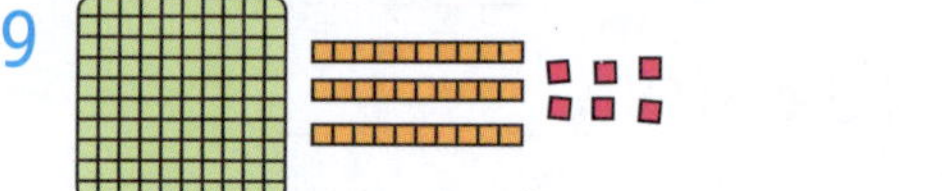 ______

10 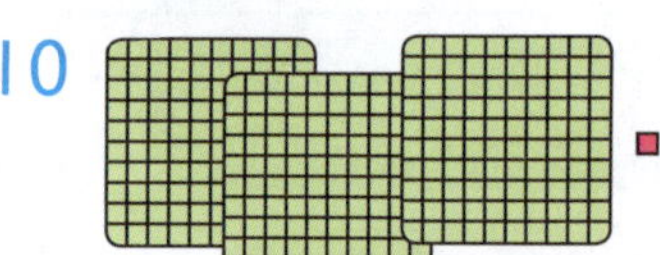 ______

Score

**B**

1 4 + 4 = ______

2 3 + 3 = ______

3 2 + 2 = ______

4 5 + 5 = ______

5 10 + 10 = ______

6 3 + 7 = ______

7 5 + 1 = ______

8 10 − 5 = ______

9 10 − 6 = ______

10 9 − 3 = ______

Score

**C**

1 $13 + $4 = ______

2 $15 + $3 = ______

3 $10 + $10 = ______

4 $14 − $6 = ______

5 $12 − $7 = ______

Complete.

6 2 + ______ = 5

7 0 + ______ = 5

8 4 + ______ = 5

9 1 + ______ = 5

10 3 + ______ = 5

Score

## Strategy
Finding halves

Half of 6 is the same as 6 ÷ 2.

Half of 6 = 3

1 half of 2 = ______

2 half of 4 = ______

3 half of 8 = ______

4 half of 10 = ______

5 half of 12 = ______

6 half of 20 = ______

7 half of 16 = ______

8 half of 14 = ______

Score

## Capacity

This bottle holds 2 cups.

How many cups in:

1 2 bottles? ______

2 3 bottles? ______

This bottle holds 3 cups

How many cups in:

3 2 bottles? ______

4 4 bottles? ______

## Area

What is the area in squares?

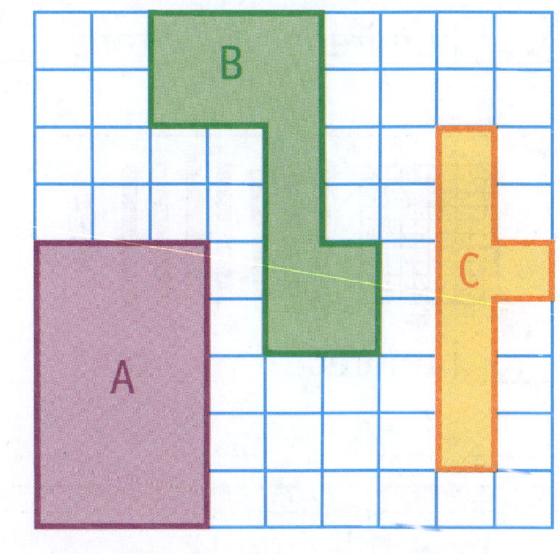


1 A ______ 2 B ______ 3 C ______

## Problem of the week

The football club wanted a blue, red and yellow jumper. Draw more jumpers and colour to show all the combinations.

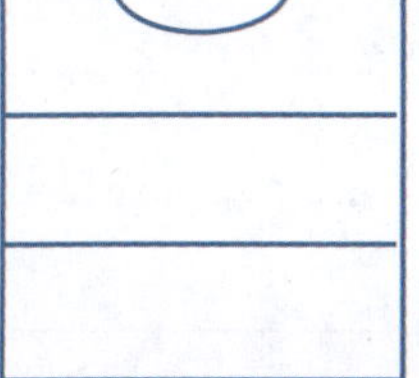

# Unit 20

**A** Continue each pattern.

1. 2, 4, 6, ◯, ◯, ◯
2. 5, 10, 15, ◯, ◯, ◯
3. 0, 3, 6, ◯, ◯, ◯
4. 50, 55, 60, ◯, ◯, ◯
5. 18, 21, 24, ______, ______
6. 20, 22, 24, ______, ______
7. 12, 15, 18, ______, ______
8. 25, 30, 35, ______, ______
9. 30, 32, 34, ______, ______
10. 40, 45, 50, ______, ______

Score

**B**

1.

______ hundreds ______ tens ______ ones

______ + ______ + ______ = ______

2.

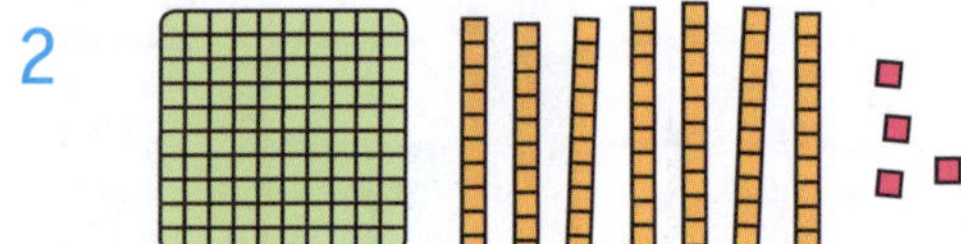

______ hundreds ______ tens ______ ones

______ + ______ + ______ = ______

3. 300 + 90 + 1 = ______
4. 700 + 30 + 6 = ______
5. 800 + 0 + 9 = ______
6. 900 + 80 + 3 = ______
7. 100 + 60 + 0 = ______
8. 500 + 0 + 7 = ______
9. 900 + 90 + 9 = ______
10. 400 + 40 + 5 = ______

Score

**C** Draw tally marks.

1. 3 ______________
2. 9 ______________
3. 16 ______________
4. 11 ______________
5. 20 ______________

Write the total.

6. ______
7. ______
8. ______
9. ______
10. ______

Score

# Unit 20

## Strategy
Looking for patterns

eg 0, 3, 6, 9, 12
pattern: +3

1 2, 4, 6, ______, ______
2 5, 10, 15, ______, ______
3 10, 20, 30, ______, ______
4 50, 40, 30, ______, ______
5 12, 9, 6, ______, ______
6 20, 18, 16, ______, ______
7 100, 90, 80, ______, ______
8 12, 15, 18, ______, ______

Score

## Data

Use the tally to complete the graph.

| Colour | Tally | Total |
|---|---|---|
| black | IIII | |
| blonde | ~~IIII~~ II | |
| brown | ~~IIII~~ III | |

## Space

How many?

1
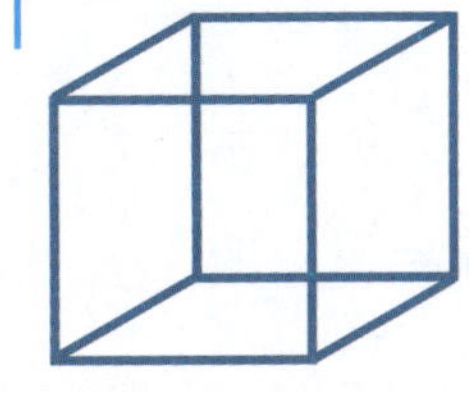

faces ______
corners ______
edges ______

2
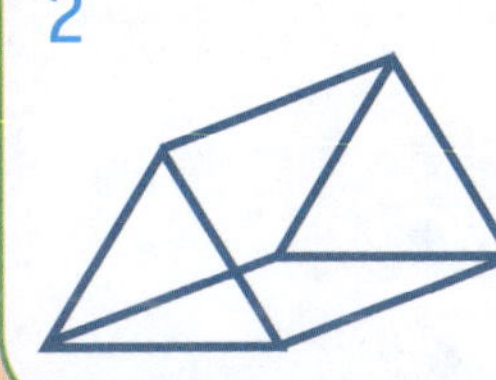

faces ______
corners ______
edges ______

## Problem of the week

Scott got $1.50 a day pocket money. Chin Ho got $10 a week pocket money.

At the end of 3 weeks who had more money? ______

By how much? ______

# Unit 21

**A** How many to make 10?

1. 8 ______
2. 5 ______
3. 9 + 3 = ______
4. 8 + 7 = ______
5. 6 + 5 = ______
6. 2 + 9 + 8 = ______
7. 8 + 12 + 3 = ______
8. 15 + 5 + 8 = ______

How much for both?

9. ______ + ______ = ______

10. ______ + ______ = ______

Score

**B**

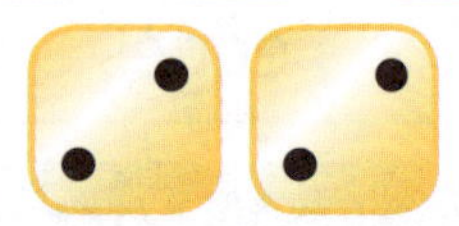

1. 3 × 2 = ______
2. 5 × 2 = ______
3. 2 × 2 = ______
4. 4 × 2 = ______
5. 10 × 2 = ______

Circle the one that weighs more.

6. a car or a bike
7. a table or a chair
8. a phone book or an egg
9. a mouse or an elephant
10. a shoe or a pencil

Score

## Strategy
Looking for patterns

eg $8 - 2 = 6$ $\quad 18 - 2 = 16$ $\qquad 9 - 4 = 5$ $\quad 19 - 4 = 15$

1. $7 - 3 =$ ______
   $17 - 3 =$ ______
2. $4 - 2 =$ ______
   $14 - 2 =$ ______
3. $9 - 6 =$ ______
   $19 - 6 =$ ______
4. $2 - 1 =$ ______
   $12 - 1 =$ ______
5. $8 - 3 =$ ______
   $18 - 3 =$ ______
6. $9 - 3 =$ ______
   $19 - 3 =$ ______

Score

## Chance

Write impossible or possible.

1. It will rain today. ______
2. You will turn green. ______
3. You will laugh. ______
4. You will blink. ______

## Symmetry

Colour to make symmetrical.

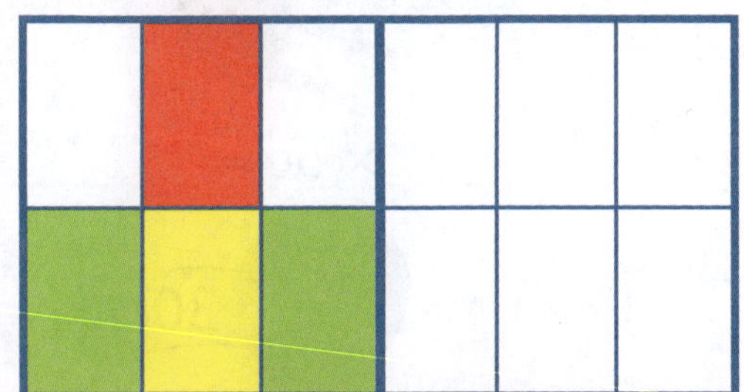

## Space

What am I?

I have:

4 straight sides

2 sides that are parallel and two sides that are not parallel.

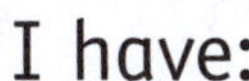

______

## Problem of the week

| 65 | 66 | 67 | 68 |
|---|---|---|---|
| 75 | 76 | 77 | 78 |
| 85 | 86 | 87 | 88 |
| 95 | 96 | 97 | 98 |

Start (97)

Where am I?

Go to start.

Go up 1.

Go left 2.

Go up 2.

Go right 2.

Go down 1.

I am on ______.

# Unit 22

**A**

1 2 × 5 = ______

2 4 × 5 = ______

3 8 × 5 = ______

4 5 × 5 = ______

5 10 × 5 = ______

6 3 × 5c = ______

7 5 × 5c = ______

8 10 × 5c = ______

9 8 × 5c = ______

10 2 × 5c = ______

Score

**B** How many 5c would you need?

1 

______ × 5c = ______

2 

______ × 5c = ______

3 

______ × 5c = ______

4 

______ × 5c = ______

Score

**C** Add.

1 6 + 5 + 4 = ______

2 2 + 9 + 8 = ______

3 7 + 3 + 4 = ______

4 4 + 3 + 16 = ______

5 6 + 10 + 10 = ______

How much is left from $10?

6 

______

7 

______

8 

______

9 

______

10 $5 ______

Score

## Strategy
### Multiplication pairs

eg $3 \times 2 = 2 \times 3$

1 $3 \times 4 =$ ____________

2 $2 \times 5 =$ ____________

3 $4 \times 5 =$ ____________

4 $2 \times 10 =$ ____________

5 $6 \times 2 =$ ____________

6 $3 \times 10 =$ ____________

7 $6 \times 5 =$ ____________

8 $8 \times 3 =$ ____________

Score

## Length

Join the length to the food.

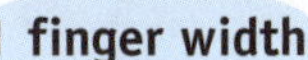

1 finger width

1 handspan

1 arm length

## 3D shapes

Name the shape of the face.

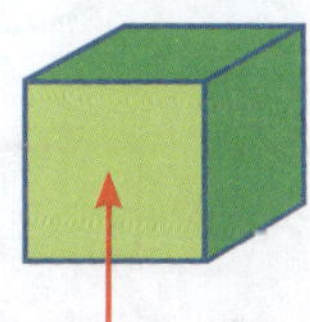

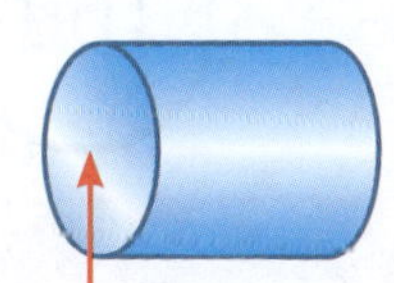

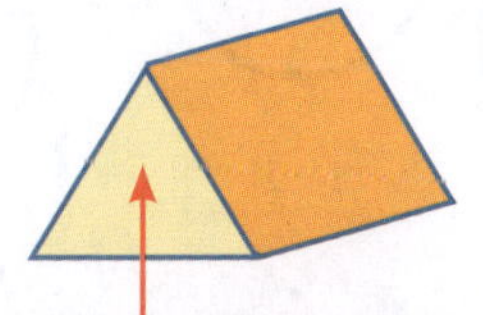

square
circle
rectangle
triangle

## Problem of the week

Nina is 10 years old. Her mother is 25 years older. Her grandmother is 63 years older than Nina.

How old is Mum? ________ Gran? ________

What is the difference in age between Mum and Gran? ________

# Unit 23

## A

Continue each pattern.

| | | | | | | |
|---|---|---|---|---|---|---|
| 1 | 1 | 3 | 5 | | | |
| 2 | 4 | 7 | 11 | | | |
| 3 | 6 | 11 | 16 | | | |
| 4 | 15 | 18 | 21 | | | |
| 5 | 31 | 33 | 35 | | | |

What is the rule?

6 13 16 19 22 25 ________

7 21 26 31 36 41 ________

8 15 17 19 21 23 ________

9 20 22 24 26 28 ________

10 9 14 19 23 28 ________

Score

## B

Colour the even numbers red, the odd numbers yellow.

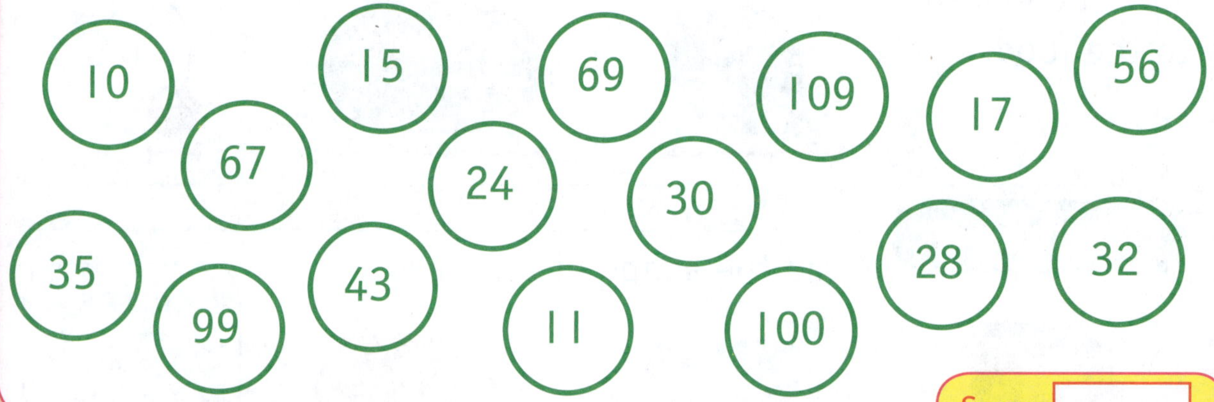


Score

## C

1 4 + 5 = ________

2 6 + 7 = ________

3 9 + 8 = ________

4 8 + 7 = ________

5 20 + 21 = ________

What is the value of:

6 the 3 in 63? ________

7 the 1 in 104? ________

8 the 6 in 263? ________

9 the 9 in 947? ________

10 the 2 in 824? ________

Score

## Strategy

Near doubles

Think doubles.

6 + 7 = 6 + 6 + 1
= 13

9 + 10 = 10 + 10 − 1
= 19

1 4 + 3 = ______

2 2 + 3 = ______

3 5 + 4 = ______

4 8 + 7 = ______

5 7 + 6 = ______

6 5 + 6 = ______

7 9 + 10 = ______

8 11 + 10 = ______

Score

## Volume

Finish the description.

1 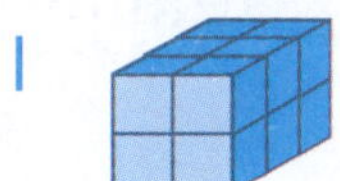

_____ layers of _____ blocks

= _____ blocks

_____ layers of _____ blocks

= _____ blocks

## Position

Draw:

a bird above the table.

a dog next to the table.

a cat on the table.

a snail under the table.

## Problem of the week

Draw more squares.

Each has to have a different number of dots in the middle.

How many did you draw?

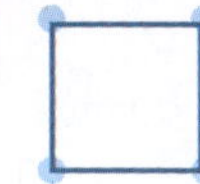

**A**

1 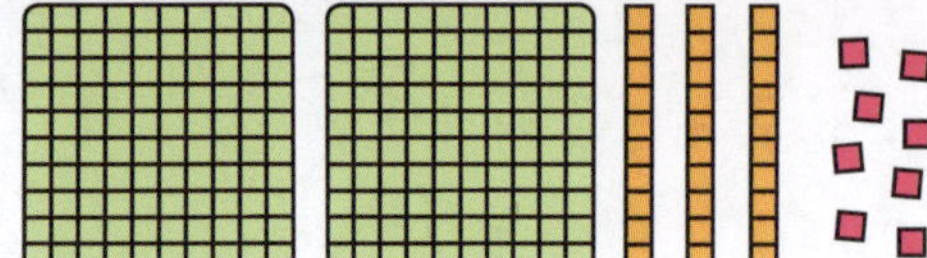

______

  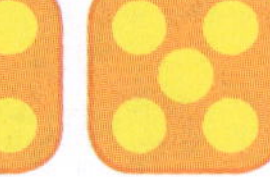

2 2 × 5 = ______

3 4 × 5 = ______

4 Write in words.

350 ______________________

______________________

5 Write in numerals.

seven hundred and twenty

______

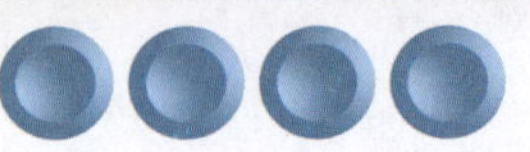

6 $\frac{1}{4}$ of ______ is ______

7 $\frac{1}{4}$ of ______ is ______

How many can you buy?

8  10c ______ stamps

9  20c ______ stamps

10 How much?

3 × 5c = ______

Score

**B**

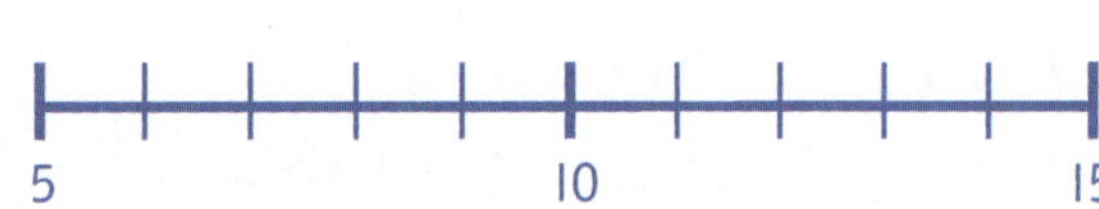

1 8 + 6 = ______

2 9 + 4 = ______

3 6 + 2 + 4 = ______

4 2 + 9 + 8 = ______

5 9 + 18 + 2 = ______

6 ______ + ______ = ______

7 ______ + ______ = ______

8 ______ − ______ = ______

9 ______ − ______ = ______

Continue the pattern.

10 0, 3, 6, ______, ______, ______

Score

## Strategy

Use the strategies you have learnt.

1 3, 6, 9, ______, ______

2 5, 10, 15, ______, ______

3 4 + 3 = ______

4 8 + 7 = ______

5 18 + 10 = ______

6 14 + 10 = ______

7 7 − 3 = ______

17 − 3 = ______

8 4 − 2 = ______

14 − 2 = ______

9 half of 10 = ______

10 10 × 10c = ______

Score

## Symmetry

Draw the line of symmetry.

1 M

2 T

3 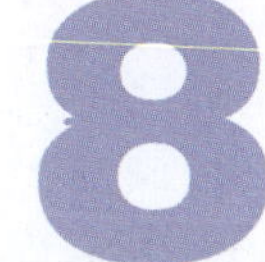

4 3

## Time

1 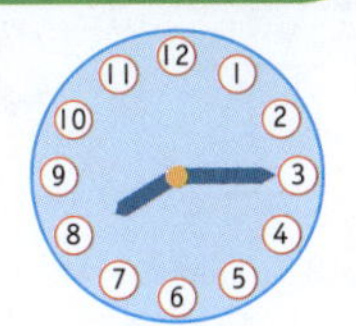

2 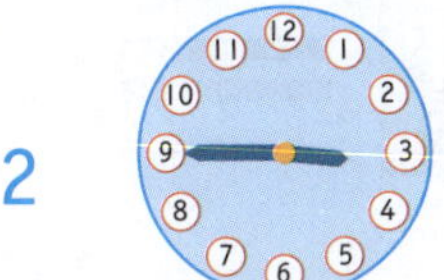

## Space

Match.

trapezium

rhombus

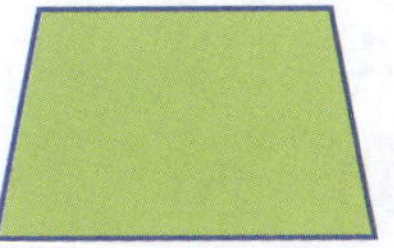

## Area

Which shape has:

1 the smallest area? ______

2 the largest area? ______

# Unit 25

**A** Complete. Look for the pattern.

1 5 + 3 = ______

15 + 3 = ______

25 + 3 = ______

2 7 + 2 = ______

17 + 2 = ______

27 + 2 = ______

3 3 + 3 = ______

13 + 3 = ______

23 + 3 = ______

How many?

4 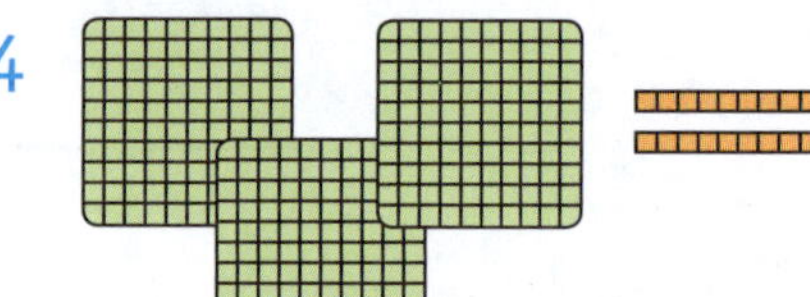 ______

5 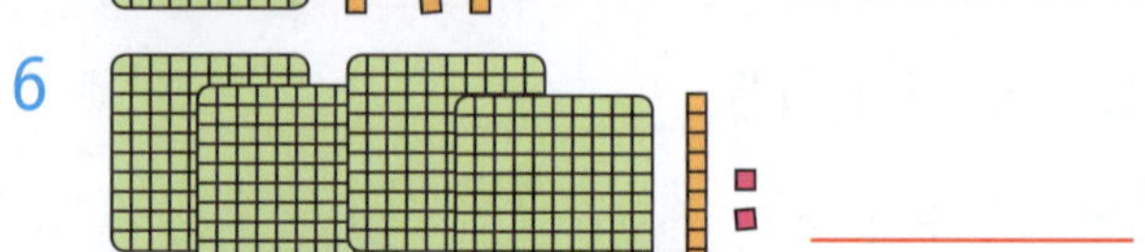 ______

6 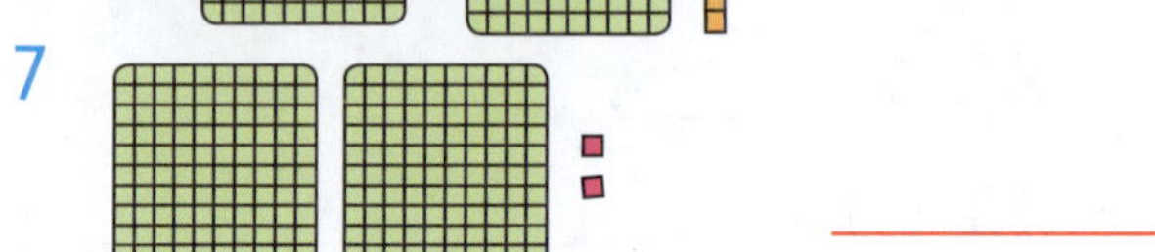 ______

7 ______

How many cents?

8  ______ c

9  ______ c

10  ______ c

Score

**B** Circle the larger number.

1 761 456

2 351 531

Circle the smaller number.

3 156 836

4 950 720

Write the number.

6 600 30 3 ______

7 800 50 1 ______

8 500 90 9 ______

9 900 10 3 ______

10 200 20 7 ______

Score

# Unit 25

## Strategy
Counting in 100s

eg 100, 200, 300, 400

500, 400, 300, 200

1 200, 300, ______, ______

2 500, 600, ______, ______

3 637, 737, ______, ______

4 700, 800, ______, ______

5 1 000, 900, ______, ______

6 400, 300, ______, ______

7 756, 656, ______, ______

8 988, 888, ______, ______

Score

## Length

How long?

1 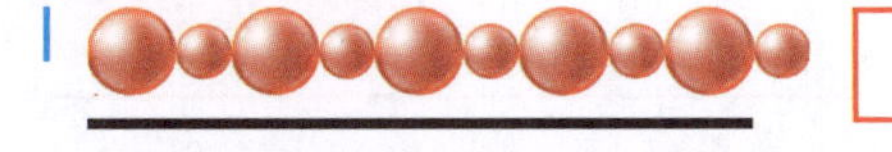

2 

3 

## Time

Complete the clocks.

The fun run: __ : __

begins at 8 o'clock.

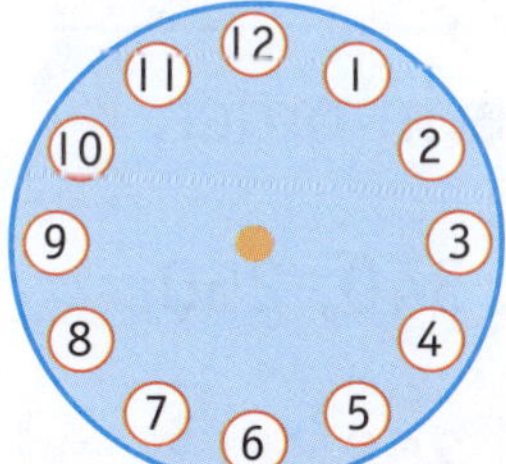

__ : __

ends at 10 o'clock.

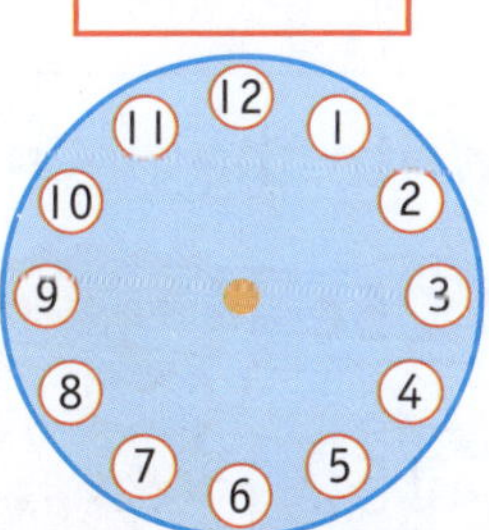

## Problem of the week

Pina and Sun Hee have 12 marbles between them. How many could they have each? eg 6, 6

______ ______ ______ ______ ______ ______ ______

# Unit 26

**A**

1 3 + 3 = ______
2 6 + 6 = ______
3 9 + 9 = ______
4 5 + 5 = ______
5 10 + 10 = ______

6 $10 + $10 = $______
7 $15 + $15 = $______
8 $6 + $6 = $______
9 $20 + $20 = $______
10 $14 + $14 = $______

Score

**B** Write the ordinal number.

1 first ______
2 eighth ______
3 fourth ______
4 third ______
5 eleventh ______

Write the word.

6 2nd ______
7 9th ______
8 7th ______
9 5th ______
10 13th ______

Score

**C** Write the new price.

1 25c 5c off ______
2 15c 5c off ______
3 60c 10c off ______
4 80c 10c off ______
5 $1 10c off ______

Write in order.

6 100, 340, 250, ____, ____, ____
7 960, 268, 117, ____, ____, ____
8 608, 306, 630, ____, ____, ____
9 282, 830, 145, ____, ____, ____
10 890, 980, 908, ____, ____, ____

Score

## Strategy

**Looking for 10**

Look for two numbers that add to 10.

eg $8 + 6 + 2 = 10 + 6$
$= 16$

1 $3 + 6 + 4 =$ ______

2 $5 + 4 + 5 =$ ______

3 $7 + 6 + 3 =$ ______

4 $2 + 5 + 8 =$ ______

5 $9 + 5 + 1 =$ ______

6 $4 + 8 + 6 =$ ______

7 $5 + 9 + 5 =$ ______

8 $3 + 4 + 7 =$ ______

Score

## Graphing

A coin was rolled 10 times.
Heads came up 6 times.
Tails came up 4 times.
Graph the results.
Write the labels.

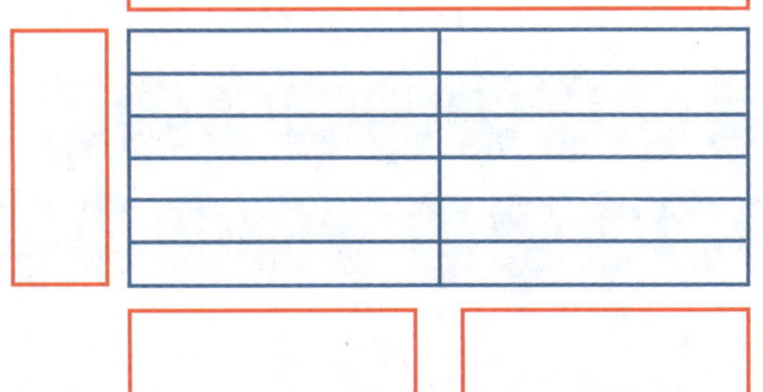

## Time

Fill in the missing months.

| January | | March | |
|---|---|---|---|
| | June | | August |
| | | November | |

## Problem of the week

The tortoise ate lettuce leaves each day.

How many did he eat in the 5 days? ______

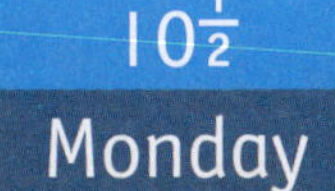

| $10\frac{1}{2}$ | $8\frac{1}{4}$ | $11\frac{1}{2}$ | $9\frac{1}{2}$ | $6\frac{1}{4}$ |
|---|---|---|---|---|
| Monday | Tuesday | Wednesday | Thursday | Friday |

# Unit 27

**A** Circle two equal halves.

1 ________ is half of 8.

2 ________ is half of 10.

3 $\frac{1}{2}$ of 20 = ________

4 $\frac{1}{2}$ of 12 = ________

5 $\frac{1}{2}$ of 16 = ________

6 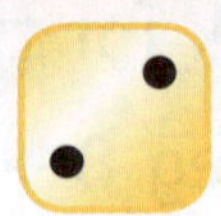   

one quarter of 8 = ________

7 $\frac{1}{4}$ of 4 = ________

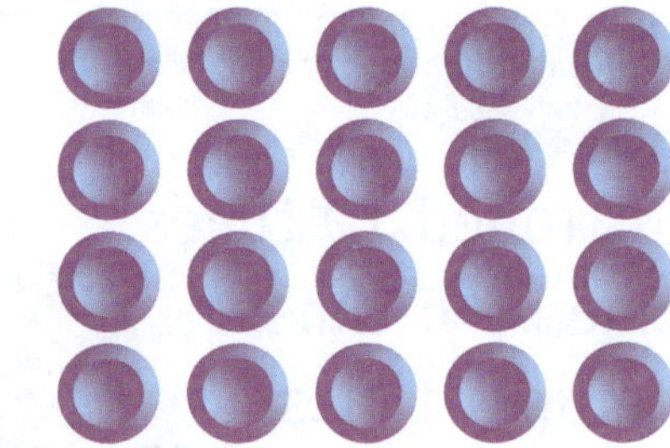

8 $\frac{1}{4}$ of 20 = ________

9 $\frac{1}{4}$ of 12 = ________

10 $\frac{1}{4}$ of 16 = ________

Score

**B** Write 679 in words. ________________________________

**C** How many cents?

1  = ________

2 = ________

3 = ________

4 = ________

5 = ________

What is their difference?

6 14 , 19 ________

7 100 , 103 ________

8 27 , 34 ________

9 89 , 93 ________

10 21 , 11 ________

Score

## Strategy
Counting in 100s

eg 100 200 300 400 etc.
136 236 336 436 etc.

Add 100.

| | | | | | |
|---|---|---|---|---|---|
| 1 | 200 ______ | 5 | 613 ______ | 9 | 500 ______ |
| 2 | 340 ______ | 6 | 720 ______ | 10 | 103 ______ |
| 3 | 473 ______ | 7 | 856 ______ | 11 | 888 ______ |
| 4 | 599 ______ | 8 | 900 ______ | 12 | 72 ______ |

Score

## Subtraction

1

Austin eats 6. Bud eats 8.

How many biscuits left? ______

2

Cathy eats 5. Jo eats 11.

How many lollies left? ______

## Time

**Paul's morning**

| | |
|---|---|
| get up | 7:00 |
| have breakfast | 7:30 |
| get dressed | 8:00 |
| go to school | 9:00 |

Write your morning times.

| | |
|---|---|
| get up | : |
| have breakfast | : |
| get dressed | : |
| go to school | : |

## Problem of the week

Chips cost 40c and drinks cost 30c. I spent exactly $1.70.

What did I buy? ______

# Unit 28

**A**

10 more.

1 30 ________
2 90 ________
3 77 ________
4 53 ________
5 $20 ________

100 less.

6 1000 ________
7 200 ________
8 500 ________
9 800 ________
10 900 ________

100 more.

11 400 ________
12 900 ________
13 600 ________
14 100 ________
15 500 ________

Score

**B** Write each number.

1 ten ________
2 forty ________
3 eighteen ________
4 one hundred ________
5 four hundred and twenty-one ________
6 ninety-four ________

Write in words:

7 75 ________________________________
8 999 ________________________________

Score

**C**

1 $\frac{1}{2}$ of $2 = ________
2 $\frac{1}{2}$ of 1 dozen = ________
3 cents in $2 = ________
4 cents in $1.25 = ________
5 double $8 = ________
6 $2 × 3 = ________
7 days in 2 weeks = ________
8 weeks in 1 fortnight = ________
9 $10 – $5.50 = ________
10 $20 – $16 = ________

Score

## Strategy

Looking for patterns

eg 0, 5, 10, 15, 20
Pattern: +5

1 20, 25, 30, ______, ______

2 50, 55, 60, ______, ______

3 35, 40, 45, ______, ______

4 1, 6, 11, ______, ______

5 13, 16, 19, ______, ______

6 7, 13, 19, ______, ______

7 10, 14, 18, ______, ______

8 21, 24, 27, ______, ______

Score

## Mass

1 The orange weighs ______ pebbles.

2 The __________ weighs the least.

## Fractions

1 Mark had 6 golf balls. He lost half of them. How many did he lose? ______

How many left? ______

2 Lisa bought 12 eggs. A quarter of them broke.

How many broke? ______

How many left? ______

## Problem of the week

I spent $1.05 and paid with . My change was 5 coins.

What were they?

# Unit 29

**A**

0 1 2 3 4 5 6 7 8 9 10 11 12 13 14 15 16 17 18 19 20

1 There are ______ 4s in 20. 20 ÷ 4 = ______

2 There are ______ 2s in 20. 20 ÷ 2 = ______

3 There are ______ 5s in 20. 20 ÷ 5 = ______

4 There are ______ 10s in 20. 20 ÷ 10 = ______

Score

**B**

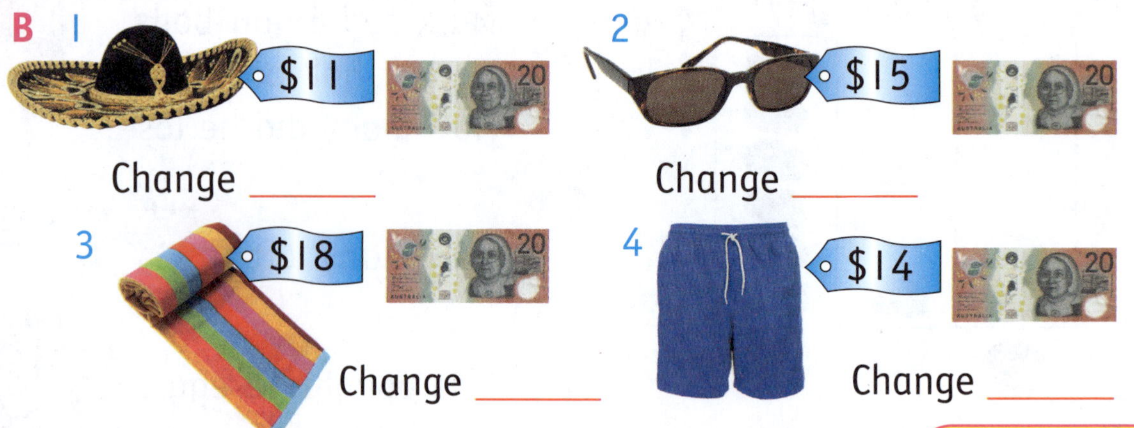


1 Change ______

2 Change ______

3 Change ______

4 Change ______

Score

**C**

How many?

1 days in a week ______

2 days in two weeks ______

3 months in one year ______

4 seasons in one year ______

5 minutes in one hour ______

Is the answer odd or even?

6 3 + 3 = ______ ______

7 8 + 1 = ______ ______

8 4 + 5 = ______ ______

9 7 + 2 = ______ ______

10 8 + 2 = ______ ______

Score

## Strategy
Making 10

eg 11 + 6 = 10 + 7
12 + 4 = 10 + 6

1 11 + 1 = 10 + 2 = ______

2 11 + 7 = 10 + 8 = ______

3 11 + 4 = 10 + 5 = ______

4 11 + 3 = 10 + 4 = ______

5 12 + 6 = ____________ = ______

6 11 + 9 = ____________ = ______

7 11 + 5 = ____________ = ______

8 11 + 8 = ____________ = ______

Score

## Volume

A

B
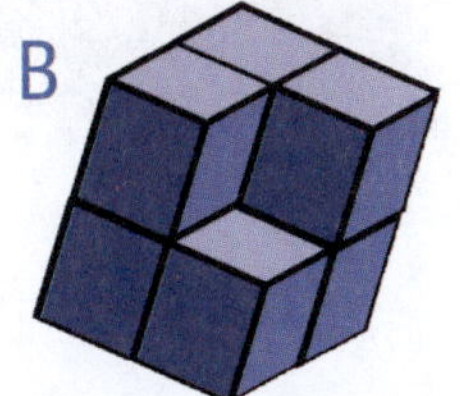

1 Model ______ takes up the most space.

2 Model ______ takes up the least space.

## Space

Circle the parallel lines.

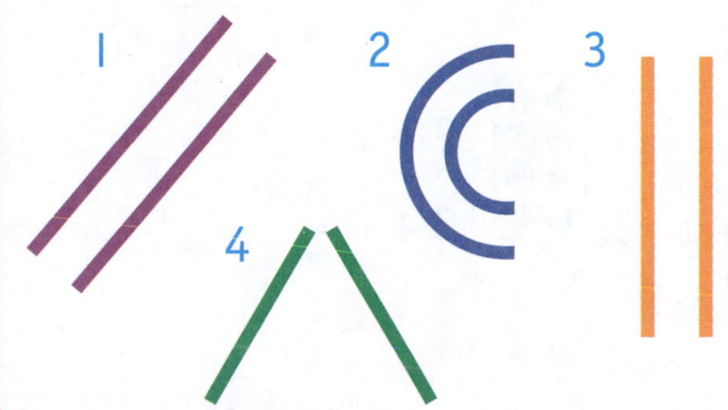


## Length

Circle the one you could use to measure time.

## Problem of the week

Bill throws 3 darts at the dartboard.

Write all the scores he could make.

| 3 | 4 |
|---|---|
| 6 | 8 |

______________________

______________________

# Unit 30

## A

1 $2 \times 2 =$ ______

2 $5 \times 2 =$ ______

3 $10 \times 2 =$ ______

4 $3 \times 2 =$ ______

5 $6 \times 2 =$ ______

6 $8 \times 2 =$ ______

7 $7 \times 2 =$ ______

8 $4 \times 2 =$ ______

Score

## B

1 $10 \div 2 =$ ______

2 $10 \div 5 =$ ______

3 $8 \div 2 =$ ______

4 $8 \div 4 =$ ______

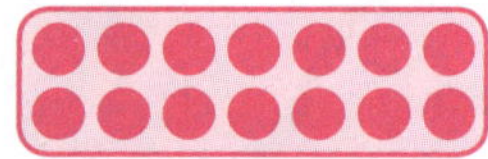

5 $14 \div 7 =$ ______

6 $14 \div 2 =$ ______

7 $12 \div 2 =$ ______

8 $12 \div 3 =$ ______

9 $12 \div 4 =$ ______

10 $12 \div 6 =$ ______

Score

## C

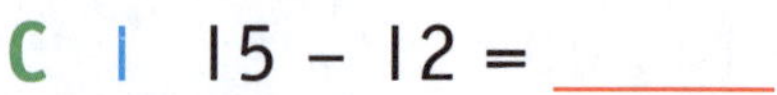

1 $15 - 12 =$ ______

2 $19 - 15 =$ ______

3 $13 - 6 =$ ______

4 $15 - 10 =$ ______

5 $8 - 3 =$ ______

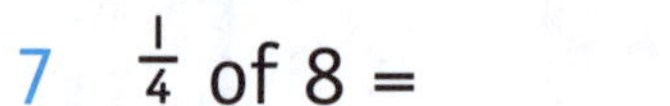

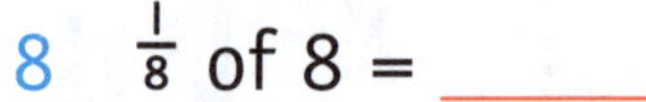

6 $\frac{1}{2}$ of $8 =$ ______

7 $\frac{1}{4}$ of $8 =$ ______

8 $\frac{1}{8}$ of $8 =$ ______

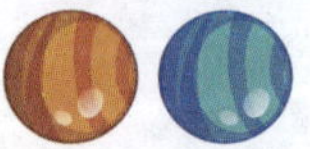

Score

## Strategy
Looking for tens

eg $6 + \overset{20}{\overline{13 + 7}} = 6 + 20$
$= 26$

Draw a line to link the tens.

1 14 + 7 + 6 = ______

2 8 + 17 + 3 = ______

3 16 + 4 + 5 = ______

4 18 + 5 + 2 = ______

5 12 + 6 + 8 = ______

6 19 + 1 + 3 = ______

7 12 + 8 + 2 = ______

8 14 + 6 + 9 = ______

Score

## Space
Draw lines to match.

1 

2 

3 

4 

cube | cone | sphere | cylinder

## Money
Draw the least number of coins to make 65c.

## Problem of the week
The number on each block is the total of the two numbers below it.

Write numbers on each block.

What is the total of all the blocks? ______

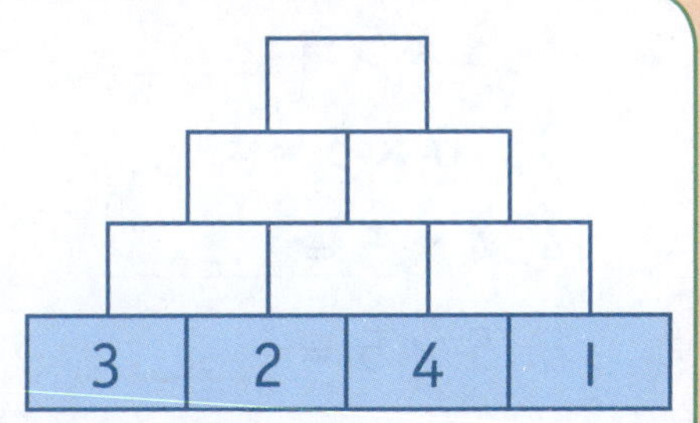

# Unit 31

**A** Divide equally.

1. 12 ÷ 2 = ______
2. 12 ÷ 3 = ______
3. 12 ÷ 4 = ______
4. 12 ÷ 6 = ______
5. 12 ÷ 1 = ______

How many stamps can you buy with 50c?

6. 25c ______ stamps
7. 50c ______ stamps
8. 5c ______ stamps

How many stamps could you buy with $1?

9. 10c ______ stamps
10. 20c ______ stamps

Score

**B** Make each pair add to 20.

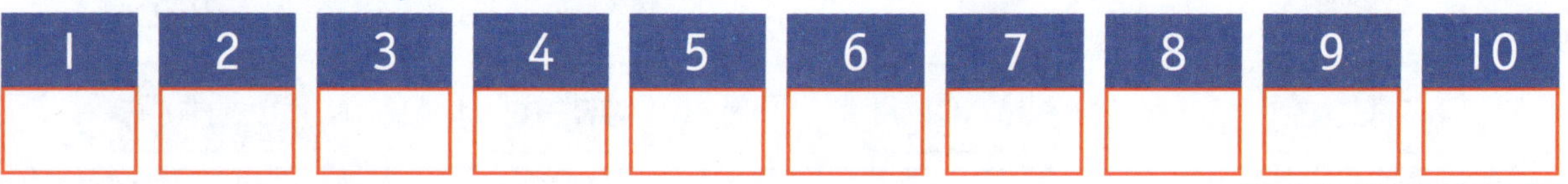

| 1 | 2 | 3 | 4 | 5 | 6 | 7 | 8 | 9 | 10 |
|---|---|---|---|---|---|---|---|---|---|
| | | | | | | | | | |

Score

**C**

1. 2 groups of 5 = ______
2. 3 × 5 = ______
3. 10 × 5 = ______
4. 4 × 5 = ______
5. 5 × 5 = ______

How much?

6. wand + mask ______
7. ice-cream + crown ______
8. wand + crown ______
9. mask + crown ______
10. ice-cream + wand ______

Score

## Strategy
Finding quarters

A quarter of 8 is the same as 8 ÷ 4.

= 2

1 a quarter of 4 = ______

2 a quarter of 12 = ______

3 a quarter of 16 = ______

4 a quarter of 8 = ______

5 a quarter of 20 = ______

6 a quarter of 24 = ______

7 a quarter of $8 = ______

8 a quarter of $20 = ______

Score

## Estimation

20 dots

Estimate ______ Count ______

## Multiplication

Write two multiplications.

______ × ______ = ______

______ × ______ = ______

## Area

Draw a different shape with the same area.

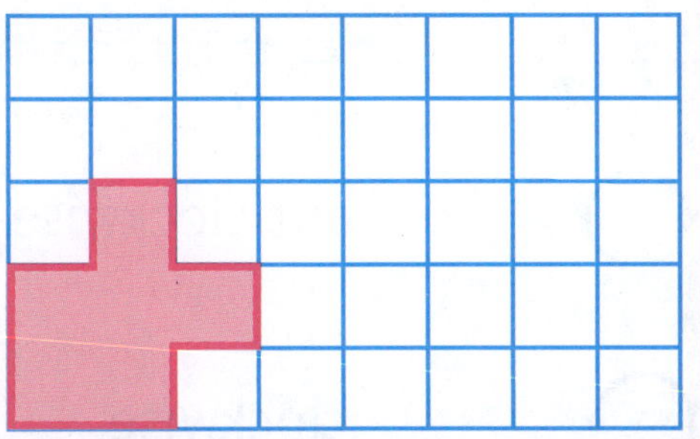

## Problem of the week

Which cricket team won?

The ____________

won by ____________ runs.

| Kangaroos | | Koalas | |
|---|---|---|---|
| Scott | 5 | Dianne | 0 |
| Justin | 20 | Bahana | 15 |
| Bruno | 10 | Juan | 5 |
| David | 0 | Cindy | 10 |
| Andrie | 0 | Boris | 5 |
| Glynn | 10 | Billy | 0 |
| Total: | | Total: | |

**A**

1 double $5 = ______

2 double $10 = ______

What is the rule?

3 1 5 9 13 ______

4 20 17 14 11 ______

5 How many cents?

    ______

6 How many?

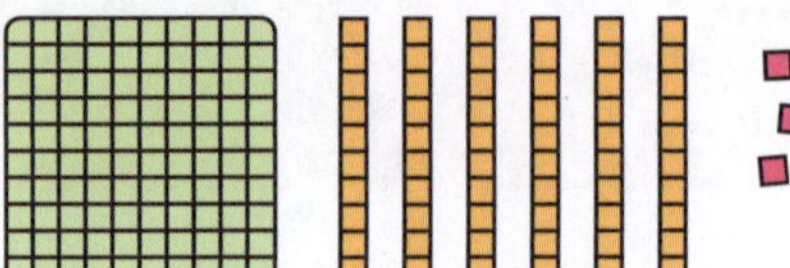

______

7 6 + 6 = ______

8 11 + 12 = ______

Score

**B** Circle:

1 the largest number.

146 641 416

2 the smallest number.

306 890 106

Is the answer odd or even?

3 4 + 4 = ______ ______

4 5 + 6 = ______ ______

5 Write the number.

700 50 8 ______

6 2 × 3 = ______

7 5 × 3 = ______

8 6 ÷ 2 = ______

9 9 ÷ 3 = ______

10 Continue the pattern.

| 1 | 4 | 7 | | | |
|---|---|---|---|---|---|

Score

**C** Clockwise or anticlockwise?

1 ______ clockwise

2  ______ anticlockwise

3 ______ anticlockwise

4  ______ clockwise

Score

## Strategy

Use the strategies you have learnt.

1 9 + 5 + 1 = ______

2 3 + 6 + 4 = ______

3 12 + 8 + 2 = ______

4 14 + 7 + 6 = ______

5

| 1 | 6 | 11 | | | |
|---|---|---|---|---|---|

6

| 13 | 18 | 23 | | | |
|---|---|---|---|---|---|

7 11 + 9 = ______

8 11 + 6 = ______

Score

## 2D

Draw the side view.

## 3D

Match.

cube

sphere

## Mass

What would you measure with these?

## Fractions

Pia had 12 cakes. She gave half of them to Joe and $\frac{1}{4}$ to Jill.

Pia gave Joe ______ cakes and Jill ______ cakes.

## Time

4:15

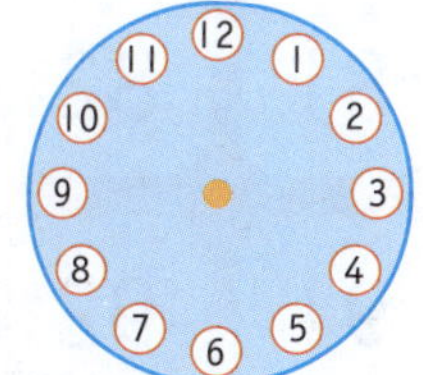


## Chance

Write a sentence using the chance word unlikely.

______________________________

# Hundred square

| | | | | | | | | | |
|---|---|---|---|---|---|---|---|---|---|
| 1 | 2 | 3 | 4 | 5 | 6 | 7 | 8 | 9 | 10 |
| 11 | 12 | 13 | 14 | 15 | 16 | 17 | 18 | 19 | 20 |
| 21 | 22 | 23 | 24 | 25 | 26 | 27 | 28 | 29 | 30 |
| 31 | 32 | 33 | 34 | 35 | 36 | 37 | 38 | 39 | 40 |
| 41 | 42 | 43 | 44 | 45 | 46 | 47 | 48 | 49 | 50 |
| 51 | 52 | 53 | 54 | 55 | 56 | 57 | 58 | 59 | 60 |
| 61 | 62 | 63 | 64 | 65 | 66 | 67 | 68 | 69 | 70 |
| 71 | 72 | 73 | 74 | 75 | 76 | 77 | 78 | 79 | 80 |
| 81 | 82 | 83 | 84 | 85 | 86 | 87 | 88 | 89 | 90 |
| 91 | 92 | 93 | 94 | 95 | 96 | 97 | 98 | 99 | 100 |

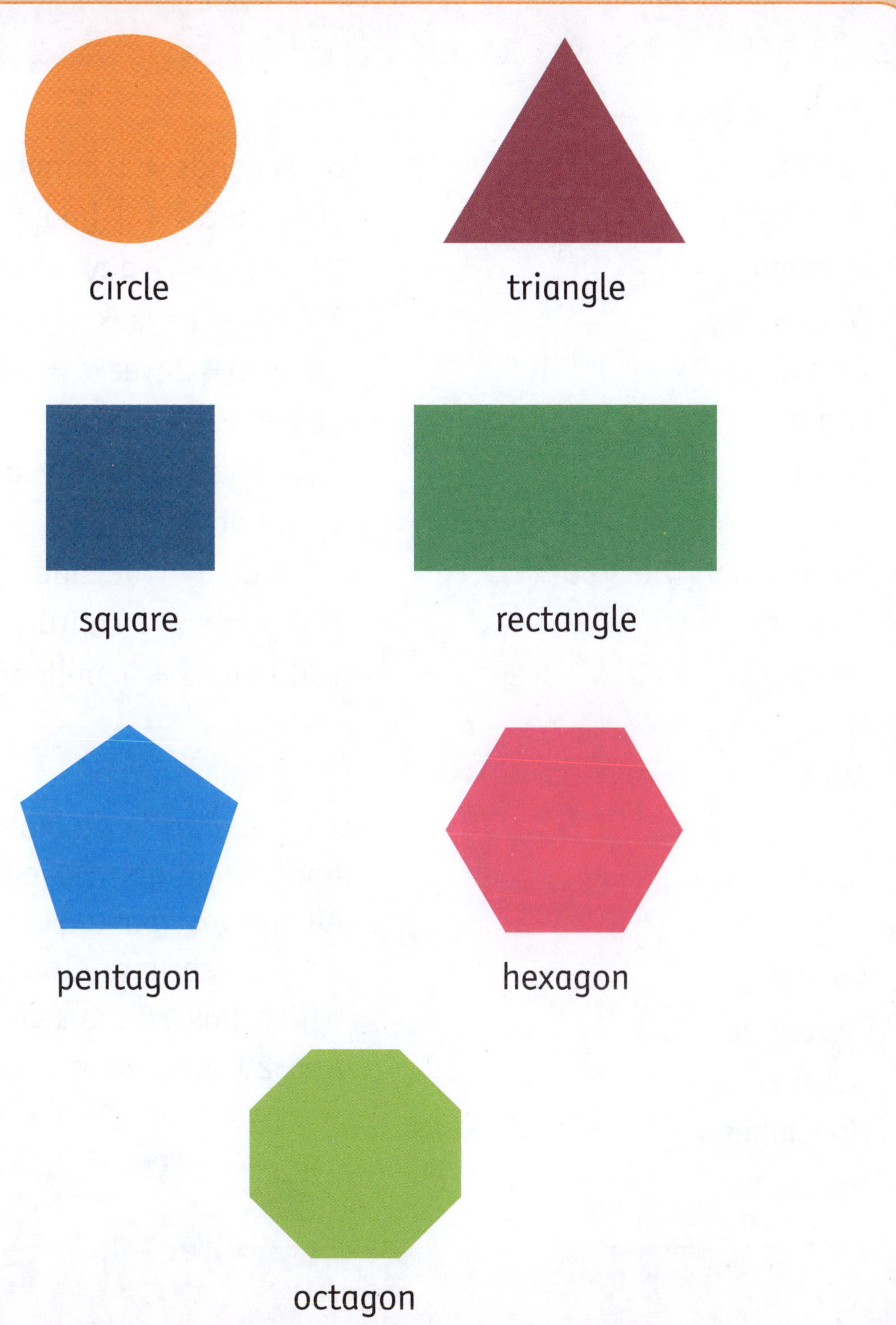
circle
triangle
square
rectangle
pentagon
hexagon
octagon

# Time

## Days of the week

Sunday
Monday
Tuesday
Wednesday
Thursday
Friday
Saturday

## Months of the year

January
February
March
April
May
June
July
August
September
October
November
December

## Time

60 seconds = 1 minute
60 minutes = 1 hour
24 hours = 1 day
7 days = 1 week
14 days = 2 weeks = 1 fortnight
365 days = 1 year
366 days = 1 leap year
12 months = 1 year
10 years = 1 decade
100 years = 1 century
1000 years = 1 millennium

## Days in months

30 days has September,
April, June and November.
All the rest have 31
Except February alone,
Which has 28 days clear
And 29 days each leap year.